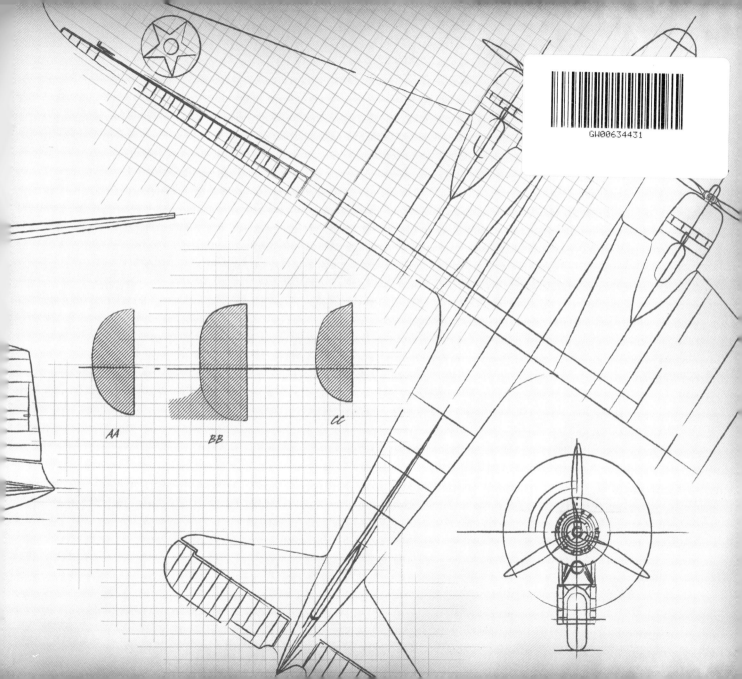

GW00634431

AA

BB

CC

This dedication is for my dearest wife Judy – who brought direction and stability to my somewhat aimless existence by becoming my wife and in consequence, my life.

Chic Eather

ABOUT THE AUTHOR

Chic Eather was born on August 2, 1920 in Sydney, Australia. In 1940, he became an anti-aircraft gunner, but was discharged while awaiting entry to the RAAF. In the interim, he joined the Merchant Navy. However, while dodging enemy submarines in the Indian Ocean, he missed his call-up and was removed from the roll of cadets.

With money he had earned as a mariner, Chic continued his flying ambitions with the Royal Aero Club, Mascot Airport, Sydney. There, in 1943, he qualified as a commercial pilot and was appointed first officer with Ansett Airways, then under government charter to the United States Service of Supply. The RAAF subsequently commissioned him as a Flying Officer, Citizen's Air Force Reserve.

In 1946, he joined the newly registered Hong Kong-based airline, the Roy Farrell Export-Import Co. Ltd., the forerunner of Cathay Pacific Airways. He flew Cathay routes from Hong Kong until 1948, when he went to Burma. During the Karen insurgency in Burma, he flew for the Union of Burma Airways. Reunited with Cathay in 1952, Chic stayed with the company until his retirement as the Senior Line Captain in 1975, having amassed 25,000 flying hours. He now lives in Queensland with his wife Judy.

OTHER TITLES BY THE AUTHOR
Syd's Pirates
We Flew in Burma
Airport of the Nine Dragons
Syd's Last Pirate (CD-ROM)

the AMAZING ADVENTURES of BETSY & NIKI

by CAPTAIN CHARLES 'CHIC' EATHER

Author   Chic Eather
Publisher   Kasyan Bartlett
Editors   Adam Nebbs and Philip Nourse
Production Manager Ronna Lau
Designer   Dennis Skouse

ISBN No: 978-988-17630-9-9

Copyright © 2008 Pacific Century Publishers Ltd
Photographs © Royal Air Force: p.30, 58, 72

The publisher would like to thank Nick Rhodes, Christopher Morgan and Jenny Lei
for their support, without which this book would not have been possible.

All rights reserved. No part of this publication may be reproduced, stored in a
retrieval system or transmitted in any form or by any means, electronic, mechanical,
photocopying, recording or otherwise, without the prior written permission of the
publisher and copyright owner.

Disclaimer
Although the publisher and writer of this book have made every effort to ensure that
the information is accurate, the publisher and writer do not accept responsibility and
hereby disclaim any liability to any party for any loss or damage arising from errors,
omissions or misleading information.

the AMAZING ADVENTURES of BETSY & NIKI

Jack "Pouch" Williams (left) and Bill "Hokum" Harris, Cathay Pacific's Chief Engineer, in front of its first engine and aircraft spares store, 1974.

This is a great story woven around Cathay Pacific's original two aircraft, Betsy and Niki; and no one is better qualified to tell the tale than Captain Chic Eather, one of the original

band of "Syd's Pirates". "Syd's Pirates" operated in a very different age and environment; they still experienced excitement, camaraderie, fun and the satisfaction of a job well done. But it was hard, exacting and, at times, dangerous work, and I reiterate that everyone involved in Cathay Pacific today

should salute those pioneers for their achievements. I believe that present-day Cathay Pacific flight crew will, as a result of reading this book, appreciate just what their predecessors endured and achieved in the immediate post-war years. There is an old Chinese saying along the lines of: "When you drink water from the well, remember with thankfulness those who had to dig the well in the first place" – a quotation very apt in the context of the remarkable story of Betsy and Niki as told in the following pages.

SIR ADRIAN SWIRE.

Roy Farrell, Neil Buchanan and Millard Nasholds, Shanghai, 1946.

CHAPTER 1 : THE BEGINNING — *In which Betsy is acquired and flown via Casablanca and various points East to Shanghai, arriving without her cargo but with a very relieved crew.*

During World War II, Roy "Pappy" Farrell and Australian Sydney "Syd" de Kantzow became friends while flying the most dangerous route in the world – the terrifying "Hump". This aerial route, from Dinjan in Assam to Kunming in western China, became legendary for replacing the fabled Burma Road that the advancing Japanese had closed by invading Burma.

Every day, in fair weather or foul (usually the latter), young pilots battled through the spurs and mountain passes of the lower foothills of the forbidding Himalayas, bringing the supplies that kept the harassed forces of China's Generalissimo Chiang Kai-shek fighting. Some of these supplies went to American General Clare Chennault's famous "Flying Tigers".

In this atmosphere of uncertain survival, Pappy and Syd mapped out their post-war future. Their plan was to sell luxury goods to the people of Southeast Asia by using a ship to import goods from the West. However, when Pappy tried to obtain a suitable vessel after the war, nothing was available. Common sense convinced him that an aircraft was a better alternative.

Betsy, arguably better known than her twin sister Niki, was born on the wartime Douglas production lines at Long Beach, USA in 1942. She was allotted the USAAC serial number 41-18385 and was finished two months later. Her military fit-out was completed at Mobile Air Depot in Alabama and she was ultimately assigned to the invasion of Europe, having survived the North African campaign.

Pappy bought C-47 No. 41-18385 for US$30,000 on October 10, 1945 from the Reconstruction Finance Corporation in Washington. Her condition at sale varied from "a real good one" to an oil-stained and

Lung Hua Pagoda in Shanghai.

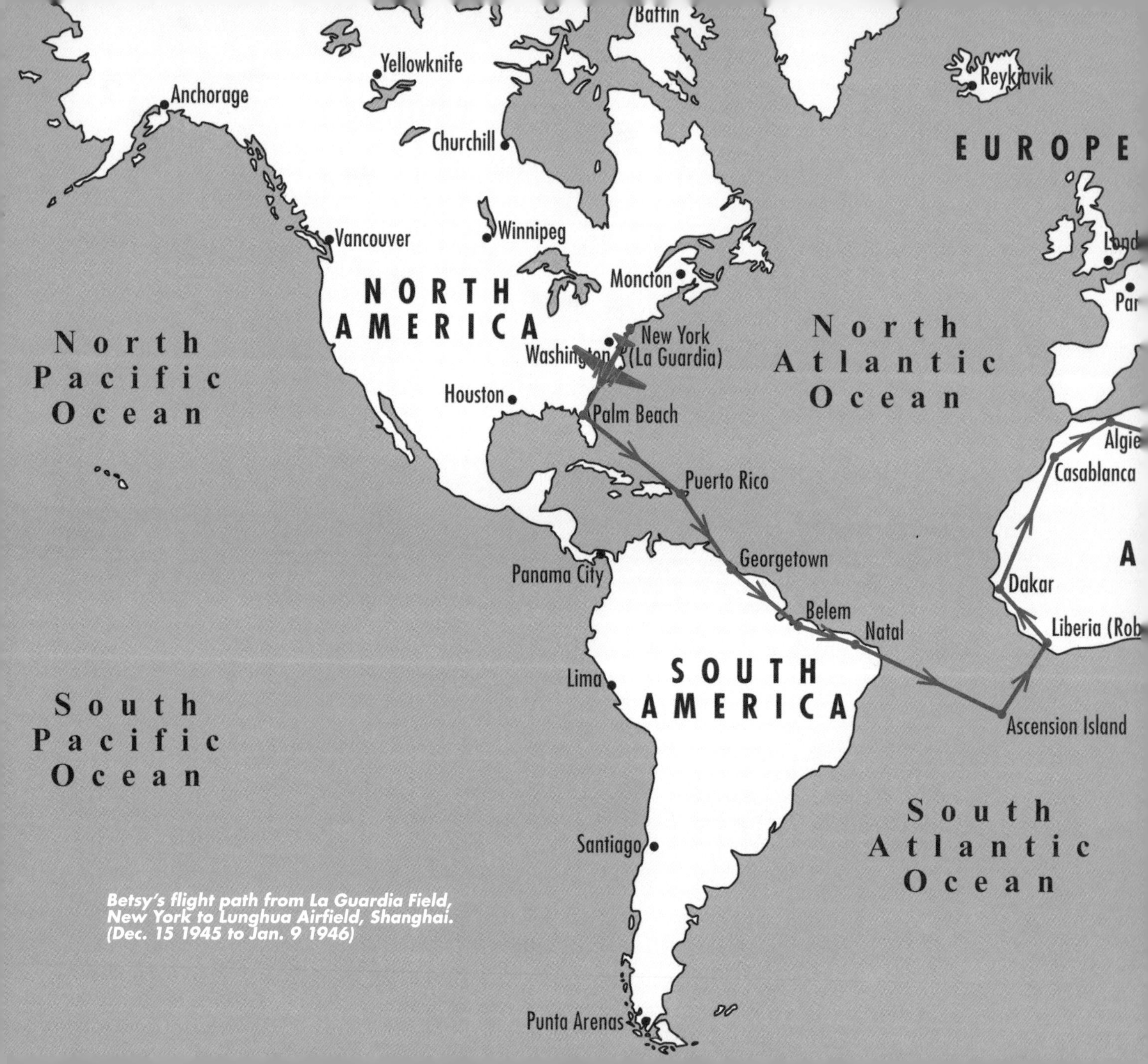

Battin

Yellowknife

Reykjavik

Anchorage

Churchill

EUROPE

Vancouver

Winnipeg

Lond

NORTH AMERICA

Moncton

Par

New York
(La Guardia)

Washington

North Pacific Ocean

North Atlantic Ocean

Houston

Palm Beach

Algie

Casablanca

Puerto Rico

A

Georgetown

Dakar

Panama City

Belem

Natal

Liberia (Rob

SOUTH AMERICA

Lima

Ascension Island

South Pacific Ocean

Santiago

South Atlantic Ocean

*Betsy's flight path from La Guardia Field,
New York to Lunghua Airfield, Shanghai.
(Dec. 15 1945 to Jan. 9 1946)*

Punta Arenas

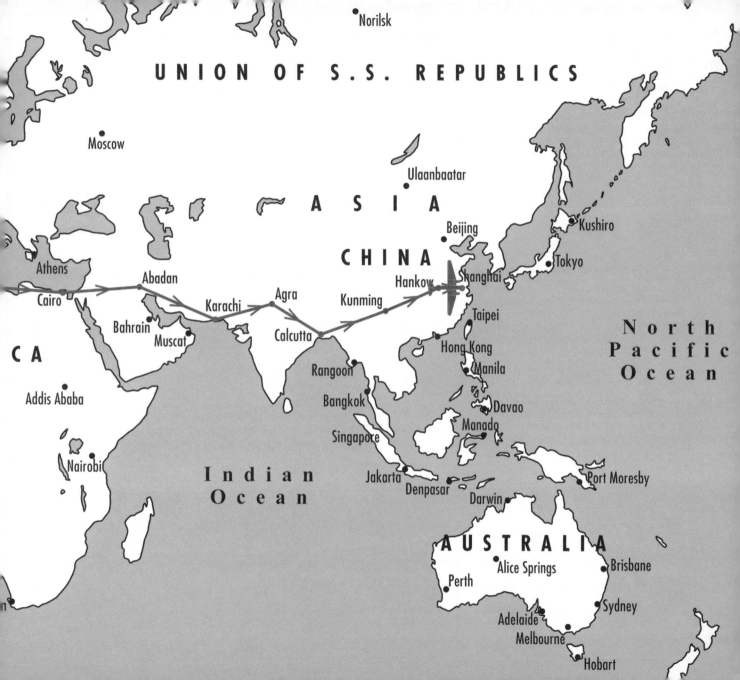

Calcutta – Betsy's last stop before reaching China.

CALCUTTA, CHITPORE ROAD

deceptively camouflaged scow of questionable antecedence and dubious age. The only general point of agreement is that a case of Johnny Walker Black Label Scotch whisky was prominent in her purchase. Yet, when Pappy first saw her, his pride of possession far exceeded his doubts. Following civilian certification, she was registered NC58093 and the story that would bring her aviation immortality as Betsy began to unfold.

The frosty dawn of December 15, 1945 had Pappy warily circling his aircraft forlornly parked outside a TWA hangar at La Guardia Field, New York. Within moments of beginning his pre-flight check, he was joined by co-pilot Robert Bob Russell. Bob latched the cargo door and followed Pappy as he clambered over a mountain of freight that filled the fuselage. The load sheet stated that they were within loading limits and correctly trimmed for Centre of Gravity. In reality, at 33,000lb the plane weighed some 6,000lb above the legal limit, and her correct Centre of Gravity was anyone's guess.

Shanghai General Post Office in the 1940's.

By the time they had taxied into take-off position, the hesitant sun had burned away the haze to visibility unlimited, and a climbing turn put them on a course for Palm Beach, Florida. They had started the long haul to Shanghai, with a diversified cargo including everything from lipstick and toothbrushes to bales of used clothing.

In the cold, crisp air, Betsy performed like a thoroughbred and they enjoyed a trouble-free trip to Palm Beach. There, navigator Bill "Ged" Geddes-Brown joined them for dinner and, realising the enormity of their enterprise, they retired early.

The next day found them en route to Borenquin Field, Puerto Rico where they refuelled. They made a technical stop at Georgetown in British Guiana, and by mid-morning of December 17 had arrived in Belem, Brazil – thoroughly clapped out. With the problem sector ahead, they headed for the sack and did not stir until Pappy woke them before dawn.

Following another stop in Natal, Brazil, the transatlantic sector was to be the decisive test, but Ged had navigated it several times as a war ferry navigator and shrugged off the dangers. In the middle of the Atlantic Ocean, he had to hit a mere dot right on the nose, and true to his ability, Ascension Island shimmered into view after several hours.

This historical street map shows the famous Shanghai waterfront or Bund and the ancient Chinese Walled City surrounded by the foreign-controlled German, French, American and British concessions - collectively called "quarters".

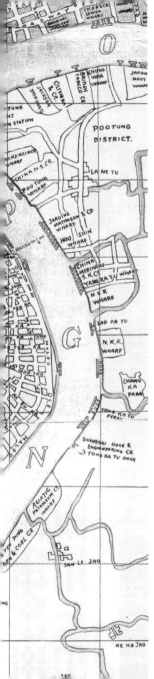

Ascension Island had become a vital Allied staging point when the German blitzkrieg overran Europe. With the fall of France, the American-based British Purchasing Commission placed massive orders for aircraft. Shipping problems combined with dismantling and reassembling slowed the delivery of these aircraft to a trickle. Beginning in June, 1941, the Allies decided to fly all planes with the necessary range from North America to the Middle East via South America, stopping off at Ascension. This was the island's greatest hour. By the time Pappy and his crew landed there, however, it had returned to a sleepy hollow, a habitat for sooty terns.

It is doubtful that the Farrell crew had such birds on their minds, and buoyed by their progress, they refuelled. Eight hours later, they touched down at Liberia's Robertsfield. They passed through Dakar in French West Africa, and then spent a day in the ancient Moroccan city of Casablanca.

Soon after the witching hour on December 23, they departed for Algiers. The breaking day found them flying an easterly course along the North African coast, while below was a scene of unbelievable war devastation and carnage, with mangled tanks and trucks littering a vast area. The crew arrived at Tripoli's Castel Benito Airport just before noon, each man gazing inwards in a thoughtful and dazed state. None of them could come to terms with the sights that they had just witnessed.

Yet more of the same awaited them as they crossed battle-hardened Tobruk and El Alamein en route to their next landing. Shortly after dark, they landed at Cairo where their request to fly on to Jerusalem was denied. They spent Christmas Day touring the Egyptian capital.

On the night of December 26, they left Cairo for Abadan in Iran, following the traditional pipeline route from Sidon to Basra. From 100 miles away, the huge oil-field flares led them to the threshold of the Abadan runway. After a quick refuelling, they were bound for Karachi, landing there before noon on December 27. The next day found them circling the glorious Taj Mahal before touching down at Agra.

Two days later, they arrived at Calcutta's Dum Dum Airport and Pappy immediately felt at home. Further problems lay ahead, however, as Calcutta was the limit of their flight authorisation. For several days, he visited the Chinese consulate, seeking permission to proceed, leaving each day despondent and mystified. On the fourth evening, a well-dressed Chinese man approached Pappy in his hotel lounge and asked him to take two young children on to Shanghai. They were the offspring of an important banking official who had sent them to Calcutta ahead of the

Niki, registered as VR-HDA, parked at Kai Tak, 1946.

advancing Japanese. With no air service from Calcutta to Shanghai, they were now stuck there and Pappy immediately agreed to take them. The next morning's pilgrimage to the Chinese consulate proved successful, and a smiling official handed him the authority to proceed into Chinese airspace. (This Chinese method of doing business was a lesson Pappy never forgot and I saw him use it to perfection many times in the Orient.)

On the January 3, 1946, this veteran of "The Hump" eased his overloaded plane up to 17,000 feet and sucked oxygen from a tube. Soon he was in a familiar environment, fighting heavy turbulence, severe icing and torrential rain. His hands moved from control to control as fast as the lightning that bolted around his plane. When the elements realised he could not be frightened, the weather suddenly cleared and the view into Kunming was glorious.

The next morning, Pappy bundled his crew into the transport, anxious to get going for the final part of the trip, but his haste was short-lived. As he opened the plane's cargo door, he found his priceless freight missing. After three days, the police had found no trace of the thieves and, on January 9, he opened the throttles and headed for Hankow.

There he found no worthwhile information about his Shanghai destination but decided to proceed. As they neared Shanghai, they intercepted a radio message that Lunghua Airfield was experiencing typhoon winds and heavy rain. Pappy told the ground operator that he had little fuel and could not divert, suggesting that the operator hold down his transmitter and he would home onto it.

Using an old Pan Am trick, he timed his legs and with wheels down and flaps fully extended, he saw to port the dim lights of the runway. He screwed left and thumped his plane onto a stormy runway. Nobody had the strength to applaud his masterly feat of airmanship. The flight was a success, and despite having no cargo to offset their costs, Pappy saw a bright spot – the kids were home!

WHAT'S IN A NAME?

As a civilian airliner it was a DC-3 — "DC" standing for "Douglas Commercial".

In American military service, with a reinforced floor and a double cargo door, it was a C-47 – officially named "Skytrain" – or, more casually, just a C-47 or a "Gooney Bird".

When supplied to the RAF it became a "Dakota" or sometimes just a "Dak" for short!

Post-war, with thousands of aircraft on the market, the venerable C-47s, Skytrains, Gooney Birds, Dakotas and Daks (and numerous other derivatives), some war-weary and some nearly new, formed the backbone of the re-emerging civil airline industry. Often, civilianised and virtually indistinguishable from one another, and regardless of their true origins, they were all referred to again simply as DC-3s – the planes that changed the world!

Junior Captains Syd de Kantzow and John 'Pinky' Wawn in their Southern Airlines (UK) uniforms, March 1939.

Jardine Aircraft Maintenance Co. Ltd, Kai Tak, 1949. JAMCO amalgamated with PAMAS in November 1950 to become HAECO.

"All that is behind us," he said. "Now let's get to work!" On February 4, 1946, under the management of Ged, the Roy Farrell Export-Import Company established itself in downtown Shanghai. With its plane based at Lunghua Airfield, the company was making money, and after several return flights to Sydney their profit margin was spectacular. This prompted Pappy to look around for an additional plane. That proved a simple task, for the Foreign Liquidation Commission (FLC) had an office on Lunghua Airfield.

In early April, he acquired from the FLC a C-47B that carried the number 44-76659. In his haste to get her working, he despatched the plane to Sydney where she ran afoul of the Department of Civil Aviation. It insisted she should be civilianised and issued her with the temporary registration VH-ASJ that was fully approved the following June. And so the legend that would become Niki was born.

It was during those heady days that Pappy made contact with his wartime friend Syd de Kantzow, who was in Australia but eager to join the action in Shanghai. Before long, John "Pinky" Wawn, Milton "Nash" Nasholds, George Peter Hoskins and other long-time friends were also reunited in the city.

Things soured for the fledgling company when a prominent Shanghai figure, who coveted its money-making possibilities, made a partnership proposition. Pappy declined the offer and from then on things only got worse: mislaid bills of lading, customs checks that caused days of delay, customs duty on items that were once free, engineering disapprovals, and so on. Finally, Pappy clandestinely loaded both his planes with engine spares and general office equipment and, under the cover of a misty dawn, left Lunghua Airfield and landed at Hong Kong's Kai Tak.

The success of the Roy Farrell Export-Import Company (Hong Kong) Limited depended on a good relationship with the Director of Air Services Mr. Albert James Robert "Papa" Moss. This proved no difficult task, for Papa, himself a rebel, had fallen in love with Syd and his "pirates". At a meeting with Neil Buchanan, Papa told him frankly that future flight approvals depended on Farrell registering both a company and its planes in Hong Kong, and so on September 24, 1946, Cathay Pacific Airways Limited was incorporated. It had a nominal capital of HK$5,000,000 in the form of 5,000,000 shares, each valued at a dollar. The directors were Pappy, Syd and

In bad weather, Chic used the junction at lower right (now Princess Margaret flyover) as his initial directional check. He then followed Argyle Street - avoiding the washing atop the police station - and 200 yards ahead lay the threshold of Runway 07.

These posters claimed the Roy Farrell Export-Import Co (HK) Ltd to be the first "Air Merchandise" service in the world.

Buchanan, and office space was leased in the premises of P. J. Lobo and Company, Chater Road, Hong Kong.

Niki and Betsy were entered on the Hong Kong Aircraft Register on October 3, 1946 as VR-HDA and VR-HDB respectively, and were the first aircraft registered since the end of World War II.

Cathay Pacific Airways' inaugural flight to Singapore via Bangkok on December 9, 1946 had standing room only. Syd arrived at Kai Tak Airport in a flurry of dust and burnt rubber to find that an enthusiastic ticket clerk, drunk on power, had sold his seat, but noting the steely glint in his managing director's eye he quickly reversed that decision. When Niki departed, Syd was comfortably strapped into his seat, and she rolled onto Singapore's Changi field right on the dot.

Roy Farrell waves from Betsy's cockpit in Sydney following what he claimed to be the first direct air service between China and Australia.

CHAPTER 2 : READY FOR TAKE-OFF — *In which I arrive at Cathay Pacific through one door, almost exit through another at several thousand feet, and discover the joys of an upholstered sewer.*

This late 1950's poster shows a CPA DC-4 above a composite Asian city.

On December 16, 1946, I arrived at the Roy Farrell Export-Import Company's office in Martin Place, Sydney. It was the hour of my destiny. A likeable fellow named Eric Kirkby ushered me into a room where two other young men were waiting. I listened as they exchanged their flying credentials. They were discharged war veterans with flying skills that made my experience resemble that of a poor relation.

Each returned from his interview beaming with satisfaction and clearly at ease. When my turn came, there sat Harry de Leuil; the same man who had once taken pity on a 16-year-old penniless youth and treated me to two flying lessons. He carefully checked my credentials and muttered that I had little to offer. When I rose to leave, he motioned me back to my seat and rechecked my logbook and references. Finally, he muttered, "In addition to a Commercial Flying Licence, you also hold a Navigator's qualification." He then pushed back his chair and walked around the room a few times, before announcing: "The job is yours."

Forty hours later, the glow of dawn painted a new day that found me at Sydney's Mascot Airport, strapped into the co-pilot's seat of Niki. With hardly a pause, Captain John "Pinky" Wawn poured on full power and an audible groan was heard as our overloaded plane left the ground. As a wide, gentle turn put us on a heading for our first refuelling stop at Charleville, my 32-year sojourn in the Orient had begun.

Carrying a cargo mostly comprised of woollen goods in 180lb bales, we progressed through Cloncurry, Darwin, Sorido, Biak and Morotai without a problem, but excitement and danger lay ahead. In the meantime, I got to know the others aboard.

22° 20'N
114°12' E

ELEV. **12** FT.

A.M.S.L.

G2 30
KAI TAK
HONG KONG

1 ° W

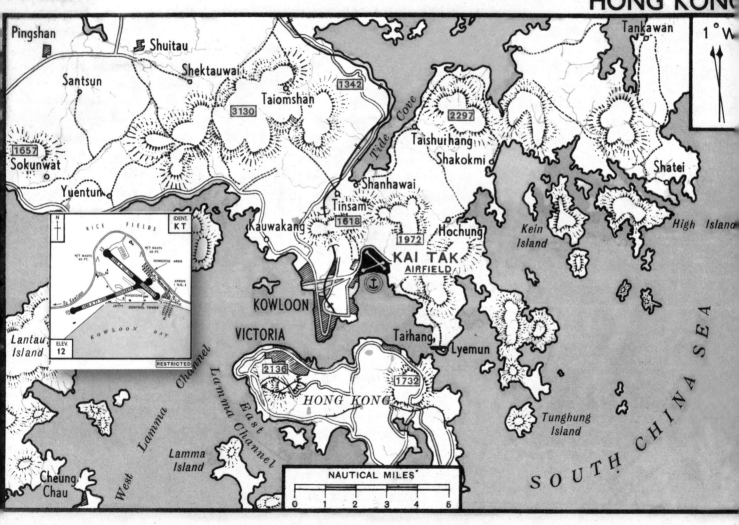

Pingshan

Shuitau

Shektauwai

Santsun

Taiomshan

1342

3130

1657

Sokunwat

Tide Cove

2297

Taishuihang

Shakokmi

Yuentun

Shanhawai

Tinsam

Kauwakang

1618

1972

Hochung

Kein Island

Shatei

High Island

KAI TAK
AIRFIELD

KOWLOON

RICE FIELDS

IDENT.
KT

W/T MASTS
40 FT.

W/T MASTS
30 FT.

DOMESTIC AREA

APRON
(R.N.)

To Kowloon

WINDCONE

JETTY
CONTROL TOWER

KOWLOON BAY

ELEV.
12

RESTRICTED

VICTORIA

Taihang

Lyemun

Lantau
Island

2136

1732

Cheung
Chau

HONG KONG

Channel

East

Lamma Channel

West Lamma Channel

Lamma
Island

Tunghung
Island

SOUTH CHINA SEA

NAUTICAL MILES

0 1 2 3 4 5

ALL HEIGHTS IN FEET ABOVE MEAN SEA LEVEL

***Kai Tak Airport,
1952 – looking west
from Tate's Cairn.
The airport looks
lazy and restful.
The visibility is
astonishingly clear
even with the cement
works in Hung Hom
adding pollutants to
the atmosphere.***

Pappy shared the co-pilot duties with me, and Lyall "Mum" Louttit was our sparks, or radio operator. The others aboard were ground engineers Bill "Hokum" Harris, Jack "Pouch" Williams and Charlie Rowe. Hokum was Cathay's chief engineer, and Pouch and Charlie became prominent in establishing the great Hong Kong Aircraft Engineering Company (HAECO). But while this was a noteworthy trio of engineering talents, Pinky's bride Kay fairly set the cabin aglow with no such qualifications.

We landed at Morotai's tiny Pitoe strip in heavy rain that endorsed its reputation for foul weather. Morotai is an island just beyond the equator at the northern tip of Celebes. To my mind, Celebes resembles a dancing elephant with its trunk in reverse. We refuelled and took off in driving rain. The thin, scorching air added to the length of our take-off and, with coconut palms flashing by perilously close, I questioned my chosen career. Finally, when fate decided it had had sufficient amusement, Pinky got us into the air, but this was only a brief respite as continuous turbulence and lightning strikes precluded boredom.

Just when a betting man would have wagered that things could get no worse, the port engine packed up. At this stage, we were an hour out of Morotai cruising at 9,000 feet, and with George doing his best to relieve our workload, I had a spare moment to realise I was probably in the wrong environment. I had assiduously studied my notes and knew that a C-47 with this sort of height would have a safe single-engine performance. True, one must expect a gradual loss of height to retain a safe flying speed, so I settled back with my book learning until Pinky's usually calm and lazy voice screeched, "I can't feather the bloody port prop." This frightened the living daylights out of me and brought me back to reality in a rush, for without a feathering capability the C-47 had the gliding inclination of a rock. This made me realise I definitely was in the wrong environment. He then added some further useful, if obvious, information: "We've lost 3,000 feet

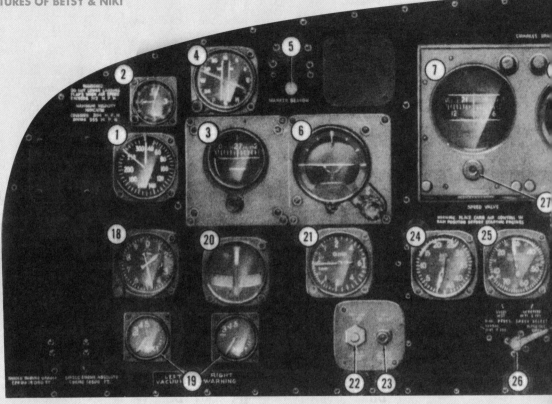

1. **Airspeed Indicator, Pilot's**
2. **Clock**
3. **Directional Gyro**
4. **Remote Indicating Compass**
5. **Marker Beacon Indicator**
6. **Gyro Horizon**
7. **Automatic Pilot Directional Gyro and Control Box**
8. **Automatic Pilot Bank and Climb Gyro and Control Box**
9. **Automatic Pilot Suction Gage**

10. **Oil Temperature Indicator (Dual)**
11. **Air Speed, Co-Pilot's**
12. **Cylinder Head Temperature Indicator (Dual)**
13. **Free Air Temperature Indicator**
14. **Carburettor Air Temperature Indicator (Dual)**
15. **Altimeter, Co-Pilot's**
16. **"WHEELS UP" Warning Light (Red)**
17. **Heating and Ventilating System Warning Lights**

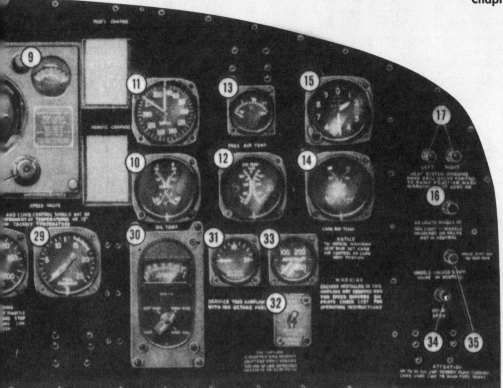

18. **Altimeter, Pilot's**
19. **Vacuum Warning Gauges**
20. **Turn and Bank Indicator**
21. **Rate of Climb Indicator**
22. **Carbon Monoxide Reset Button**
23. **Carbon Monoxide Warning Light**
24. **Tachometer**
25. **Manifold Pressure Gauge (Dual)**
26. **Manifold Pressure Gauge Selector Control**

27. **Automatic Pilot Speed Valves**
28. **Oil Pressure Indicator**
29. **Fuel Pressure Indicator**
30. **Fuel Quantity Gauge**
31. **De-Icing Pressure Selector Valve**
32. **Static Pressure Selector Valve**
33. **Automatic Pilot Oil Pressure Gauge**
34. **"DOOR OPEN" Warning Light**
35. **"WHEELS LOCKEED" Warning Light (Green)**

With sparkling eyes and boyish enthusiasm, Capt Roy "Pappy" Farrell and F/O Bob Russell begin the flight from New York to Shanghai.

and she's going down fast." I gave him the benefit of being rhetorical for the altimeter had me hypnotised. My eyeballs had recorded every lost foot.

Pinky ordered me to get back and start jettisoning the cargo, so at last I had something to do. I bounded out of the right-hand seat (proud that I had remembered to unclasp my safety belt), but was unceremoniously jerked back. The same thing had happened with Jimmy Broadbent in a sabotaged Electra when I'd forgotten the stout headset cable. My savoir-faire took a tumble. Was I learning nothing from these emergencies? As I pushed past Pappy, his face was white and strained. I wondered why! With his experience, surely this was all child's play. Then I remembered the loss of his cargo would increase the strain on his struggling company. Nevertheless, first things first! With the help of Pouch and Charlie, the door was open in a flash and we began pushing out the expensive bales. With the loss of each one, Pappy's face became greyer. Then, just as I pushed out a large bale, Niki jolted severely and I swayed through the door. To this day I swear I saw the underbelly fuselage rivets but the strong hands of my colleagues grabbed my belt and hauled me back in.

At that very moment, Pappy yelled that Pinky had feathered the prop and that the height had stabilised. As I scrambled back to the flight deck, Pouch and Charlie latched the cargo door. I could hardly believe my eyes: the altimeter read 1,500 feet. As a new boy and reluctant to make more of a fool of myself than was absolutely necessary, I stared but held my tongue. The loss of 7,500 feet is a sobering thought, and of greater interest – what if there had been no 7,500 feet to lose? That lesson stayed with me all my flying life and I never rushed my pre-flight checks.

Reaction to my close miss with disaster did not set in until some two days later. Then my overactive imagination saw visions of my portly body splashing into the shark-infested waters

FLIGHT DECK CONTROLS

1. *Left Fuel Selector Valve Control*
2. *Elevator Trim Tabs Control*
3. *Propeller Controls*
4. *Elevator Trim Tabs Indicator*
5. *Throttle Controls*
6. *Mixture Controls*
7. *Right Fuel Selector Valve Control*
8. *Rudder Trim Tab Control*
9. *Automatic Pilot "ON-OFF" Control*
10. *Rudder Trim Tab Indicator*
11. *Parking Brake Lock Control*
12. *Aileron Trim Tab Indicator*
13. *Aileron Trim Tab Control*

F/O Chic Eather, Hostess Judy Chui and R/O Dick Labrum in front of VR-HDW. Kallang Airport, Singapore, July 1948.

of the Davao Gulf. On a realistic level, the company had lost 20,000 pesos of cargo jettisoned 150 miles from Davao, and sundry items of expensive aircraft equipment. It came as no surprise when an extensive search by the authorities recovered nothing.

The reprieve of our plane was due to Pinky's recollection that the erring prop was changed in Sydney in a rush. He rightly figured it was not bled correctly. As the airstream turned the prop, he pushed the pitch lever that changed the blade angle and pressed the feather button. This proved successful.

As the used fuel decreased Niki's weight, Pinky showed his class by coaxing her up to 3,000 feet, and we later landed at the old Japanese Libby Airstrip at Davao in southern Mindanao. Pappy found us rooms at Guino's Hotel where I made the acquaintance of the biggest mosquitoes I have ever come across. Throughout the night, cables flashed to and from Manila. Pappy learned there was a spare engine at Manila and, as luck would have it, Betsy had a layover there. At first light, she brought the spare engine and immediately returned to Manila with Pinky and Mum Louttit.

Pappy advised me that he would command the rest of the flight. He added that I would continue as first officer and asked if I could handle the radio as well. I assured him I could, but said that I would like Mum to run through the frequencies I might need. He agreed and later drove me to the hotel and suggested I get a good night's sleep. He then found a carpenter to build a cradle for the duff engine. This would make the loading easy for its return to Manila.

Fishing boats in Hong Kong Harbour celebrate a local festival.

Meanwhile, with all that engineering talent at his disposal, Pappy organised a gantry and overnight the sick engine was removed and secured on the wooden cradle. When the replacement engine arrived, its installation proved a simple task. The next morning, Pappy and I made a short test flight over Libby Airfield. The replacement engine performed well and we landed. Without our cutting the engines, all colleagues scrambled aboard and we left for Manila. There followed a 20-minute stop for fuel after which Pappy taxied Niki out, lined her up and said, "Right, I want you to do the take-off."

Chic's first approach crossed the Peninsula Hotel, his future home from home. He kept Lion Rock to port and then used an ancient cemetery to line up on Runway 13. This unique painting shows the threshold of "13" just beneath Betsy's nose.

With the Chinese meteorology station on Pratas Reef slipping astern, a radio message advised that an unexpected squall line had struck Hong Kong airspace. Heavy rain and dangerous winds were hammering the area. As we approached the coast, the sky had darkened from milky grey to a sinister purple. Pappy explained that our usual approach would be on an NDB (Non-Directional Beacon) located at Hung Hom. It was on 330k and identified as KT. He added that in this storm it was useless. Then he lost altitude until we were skipping just above a gunmetal-tinged windswept sea. With Waglan Island ahead, severe turbulence hit and Pappy asked me to help him on the controls. Then, straight ahead, I saw a vertical sliver of light a quarter-mile wide, Lei Yue Mun Pass.

As we inched through the pass, the pelting rain rendered the wipers useless. Safely through the pass, we entered an unidentifiable vacuum. Pappy said: "The Harbour," his voice seeming to register more hope than conviction.

He ordered me to keep a good lookout. "For what?" I pondered. I had never been to Hong Kong before! But this seemed an inopportune moment to engage in small talk. To show I understood his order and with forced savoir-faire, I slammed open my storm window and within seconds was drenched by freezing rain. Pappy, nodding his approval, copied my action and suffered the same fate, which for some reason gave me great pleasure.

With a yell, and a vicious stab on the rudder pedal, he brought Niki around a huge Chinese junk that gave me such a clear view of the helmsman that I fancied I could read his mind. We hurled past the Peninsula Hotel at rooftop level. I saw, for a fleeting moment, a vague shadow that Pappy yelled was Stonecutters Island. As an easterly turn

Ms Iris Stoburt, Air Hostess Supervisor, Ms June Lee, Philip Chen and Captain Ken Steele at Cathay Pacific's booking office in the Peninsula Hotel.

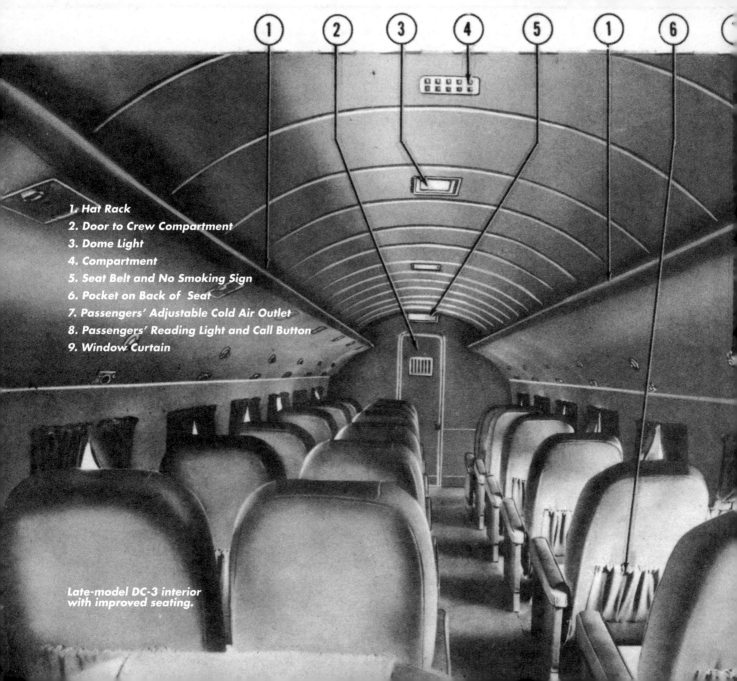

1. Hat Rack
2. Door to Crew Compartment
3. Dome Light
4. Compartment
5. Seat Belt and No Smoking Sign
6. Pocket on Back of Seat
7. Passengers' Adjustable Cold Air Outlet
8. Passengers' Reading Light and Call Button
9. Window Curtain

Late-model DC-3 interior
with improved seating.

brought us into the circuit for the runway – a circuit that must have existed mainly in Pappy's memory – my bulging eyes saw ghostly buildings dead ahead that somehow moved aside, at the last moment, to let us pass. I squirmed as a hilltop cemetery flashed beneath with the thought that the undertaker wouldn't have far to bring the broken body parts from the crash scene. Then I saw Pappy's face soften to a grin – he knew that final resting place put us onto our final approach. As Niki touched down on the water-saturated runway, he hit the brakes. I found myself hoping that the slight reduction in speed was not all imagination – I had recently read a terrifying article on aquaplaning.

With the danger over, I felt a wild exhilaration – one I would feel again and again – of outwitting the most dangerous and exacting airport in the world. Then, right on cue, out came the sun.

Pappy slowly taxied to his assigned spot and cut the engines. He looked at me, winked and said, "How do you like your new work environment?" Then, with a sigh, he suggested we had better clear the necessary requirements.

He led me along a series of precariously floating duckboards that ended at the open flap of the first of several Royal Air Force tents that were erected on the sea wall. This was the spartan accommodation from which Immigration, Health and Customs performed their duties.

As I cleared the Customs, I saw Pappy in deep conversation with Syd, who caught my eye and bounded up with outstretched hand and a smile a mile wide. Apparently, Pappy had given me a good rap. He then introduced me to Cathay Pacific's Public Relations Officer, Bill Dobson. Then with a nod from Inspector F. "Buck" Indge-Buckingham, the senior duty policeman, we walked to the centre of the airfield.

From that position, Syd gave me a concise familiarisation briefing. His finger traced the RAF Control Tower that controlled both service and civilian plane movements, and then moved to the HMS Flycatcher and the RAF establishment buildings. He pointed out the towering mountains that cupped the airport to the east and north. This he described as the Nine

Tom Bax, Cathay's Traffic Manager, arrives at Cat-Bi, Haiphong, November 12, 1949, on the first scheduled Hong Kong – Haiphong service.

Dragons – probably the best-known of which is Lion Rock. Then his finger moved to the western skyline that was relatively clear of hilly ground. He grumbled that the line of milky smoke that hid the western horizon came from local manufacturing plants. When this was mixed with low cloud, visibility was zero.

As his gaze moved left, he indicated the Peak on Hong Kong Island. Further left was an uninspiring concrete monstrosity that festered on the crest of Mount Cameron - the Japanese War Memorial. Its only redeeming feature, Syd said, was its

Cathay cabin staff give a welcoming smile in this late 1950's picture.

value to the aviator. When the afternoon sun bounced off its surface, one could pick up its glitter from Pratas Reef some ninety miles away. After adding that Mount Parker, further left, was probably the greatest danger of all, he chuckled, and said, "You already know about Lei Yue Mun Pass."

Fixing me with a beady eye, Syd snarled that I must never be party to a take-off that pointed at Lion Rock. To drive home his point, he described in gory detail the crash of an RAF flight three months earlier. Nineteen lives were lost when it crashed into the foothills of Kowloon Tong. He moved back to the seawall to a partly completed brick building. This, he stated, was to be the first substantially built post-war terminal. With a few other minor remarks, he brought the briefing to a close and stated that he would drive me to my digs. Bill, who doubtless had experience of his driving, found other business that needed his attention.

HOW FAR IS AUSTRALIA?

By rocket mail, the just-round-the-corner possibility is that you'll get a reply by tea-time to a letter despatched immediately after breakfast. In this age of scientific marvels, when Distance is shorter, the World is smaller, and Time is not so long, CATHAY PACIFIC AIRWAYS offers to you speedy reliable passenger and freight service to the key cities of the East and Australia. By CPA airliner it is now possible to leave Hong Kong after breakfast and arrive in Sydney for lunch the following day. Remember it costs less and it takes less time to-day to fly CPA.

Passenger and Freight Booking
Agents
(P. J. LOBO & CO.)
4 Chater Road.
Tel: 31161 & 31162.

AIRMERCHANDISE

IS NOT FOR SNAILS!

A MESSAGE TO BUSINESS MEN

The tempo of modern life demands SPEED and that includes SPEEDY DELIVERIES.

That is why the Roy Farrell Export Import Co., (H.K.) Ltd., makes EXTENSIVE use of the SKYWAYS in addition to the Sealanes.

To assure the public SPEEDY DELIVERIES of Priority Cargo in Time for the Season of the Year and the Market —and TIME IS MONEY.

The Roy Farrell Export-Import Co. (HK) Ltd.

The First International AIRMERCHANDISE Service In The World

402-403 York Building,   Telephones: 31350,
Chater Road, Hongkong.   31360

and at

SYDNEY (AUSTRALIA), MANILA (PHILIPPINE ISLANDS), SHANGHAI (CHINA) and LONDON (UNITED KINGDOM).

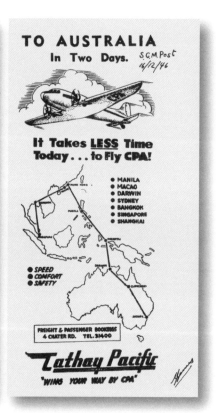

TO AUSTRALIA
In Two Days.   S.C.M. Post 16/12/46

It Takes LESS Time Today . . . to Fly CPA!

- MANILA
- MACAO
- DARWIN
- SYDNEY
- BANGKOK
- SINGAPORE
- SHANGHAI

- SPEED
- COMFORT
- SAFETY

FREIGHT & PASSENGER BOOKINGS
4 CHATER RD.   TEL. 31400

Cathay Pacific
"WING YOUR WAY BY CPA"

A series of early newspaper advertisements aiming to keep Betsy and Niki gainfully employed.

The interior of a 1960's Cathay Pacific aircraft.

Opposite page: pictures of Cathay Pacific staff.

That drive proved to be the most dangerous leg of all, with Syd weaving in and out of traffic with proprietorial disdain. Other road users seemed conversant with his methods and moved swiftly to the safe haven of the nearest curb.
I was terrified but my fixed grin seemed to project that I was thoroughly enjoying his bout with Providence and he seemed to further mellow to me. We covered the five miles in four minutes; then, with screeching brakes and the smell of burning rubber, I was deposited at the main doors of the imposing Peninsula Hotel. There the company reserved two rooms for transiting crew in what became known as the "upholstered sewer". Each room was crammed with camp beds that never seemed empty. Syd selected one that he guaranteed was full of sleep, but this luxurious accommodation lasted just two nights.

On December 23, I found myself on VR-HDG, Cathay Pacific's third C-47, on my way back to Sydney. A week later, I was back in the Peninsula Hotel, snug as a bug in a rug in my favourite camp bed. My log book shows that, during my first fortnight with Cathay Pacific, I logged 94 hours of flying time, during which time I had two days off.

With that pace, this virile company would burn me out within a month. But how wrong were those thoughts, for I thrived on what lay ahead, and for the next three decades Kai Tak was to be my home away from home.

The crew that repaired Niki following her spectacular landing in Macau. Left to Right: Chief Engineer, Bill ("Hokum") Harris, R/O W.J. (Bill) Carew and Neil Norquay. Macau, April 1947.

CHAPTER 3 : NIKI'S MACAU ADVENTURES — *In which Niki crash-lands on Portuguese soil to a live musical accompaniment.*

The then-Portuguese enclave of Macau, about 40 miles west of Hong Kong, caught Pappy's attention. He reasoned that any short-haul operation meant a plane could complete several return flights each day with no catering requirements, and the short lines of communication meant that engine or airframe problems could be quickly rectified.

A discussion with P. J. Lobo's eldest son, Rogerio "Roger" Hyndman Lobo, gained his support. However, before making an official application, he decided it was prudent to check the C-47's performance on a grass area (pre-war racecourse) at Macau.

On September 1, 1946, Peter Hoskins made several landings and take-offs from the enclave's pocket-size field in Betsy. The proving flights determined that the limited length of the grass field was feasible, but that a precise final approach speed and touchdown point was vital.

On September 20, using Peter's report as a basis, Syd wrote to Papa Moss, the Director of Air Services, Hong Kong, requesting consideration for scheduled operating rights between the colony and Macau.

Three days later, Pappy and Syd signed the Memorandum and Articles of Association of Cathay Pacific Airways, and it was incorporated the next day – September 24, 1946.

At the beginning of January 1947, Lisbon and London were still considering Cathay Pacific's application to start such a service. However, in the interim they were permitted to begin operations as a non-scheduled carrier utilising the C-47.

An official reception was planned for the inaugural flight on January 5, 1947. In Macau, local dignitaries, in the trappings of their office, keenly assembled at the end of a red carpet to watch Niki make her landing. Pinky Wawn, assisted by co-pilot Syd, had her approach speed captured to the knot.

Macau 1947. Syd de Kantzow with his wife.

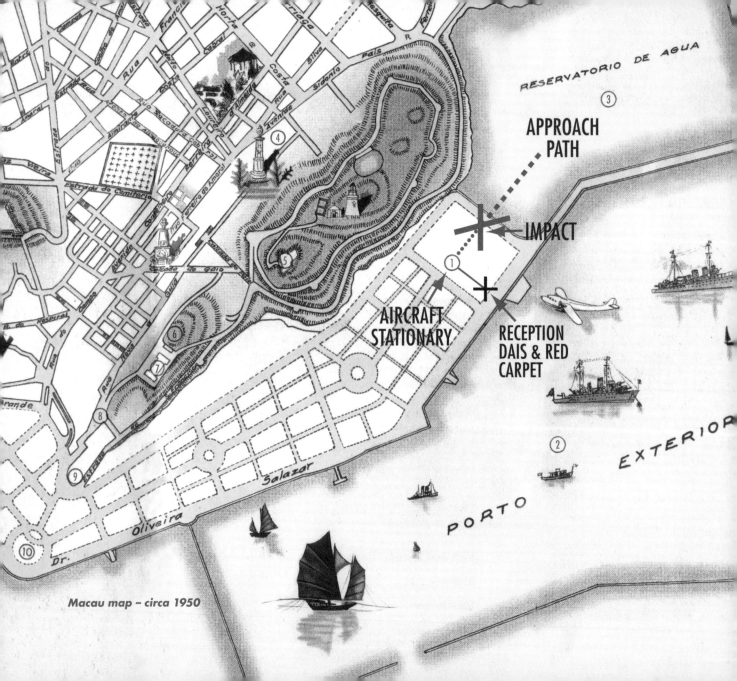

RESERVATORIO DE AGUA

③

**APPROACH
PATH**

④

IMPACT

①

**AIRCRAFT
STATIONARY**

**RECEPTION
DAIS & RED
CARPET**

⑤

⑥

⑦

⑧

②

⑨

PORTO EXTERIOR

⑩

Macau map – circa 1950

Another of the Roy Farrell Export-Import Company's partners, standing between the pilots, got a bit toey at the flat approach. He stood it until his nerve failed and with an oath he scuttled back to the cabin. His rapid retreat upset the delicate balance of the precisely flown plane and the already-extended wheels clipped the retaining wall of the reservoir.

The field lay just beyond the retaining wall of the Reservatorio de Agua, the water supply of the enclave. The strike folded back the undercarriage and Niki's props tore out great divots of earth and grass. Out of control, she slid on her belly and stopped with the cabin door lined up with the red carpet.

The door opened and a thoroughly sheepish crew stepped down. Under the impression that this was part of the show, the band's trumpet section heralded the occasion, and the spectators went wild. The crew lined up before the welcoming committee and its spokesman delivered his congratulatory address as though nothing untoward had happened. Here was savoir-faire at its blindest!

Naturally, Cathay Pacific was upset with the loss of Niki's earning capacity, as was the crew for causing the damage. The event was a blessing in disguise, however, for it clearly showed the C-47 did not suit that small field. Fortunately, the accident did not have an adverse effect on the future grant of the Macau operating rights and led to the introduction of the Catalina service.

A 1950's view of Macau's Inner Harbour, with Hong Kong steamers alongside the waterfront.

On April 20, 1947, Cathay's Hokum Harris, Bill Carew and Neil Norquay put the finishing touches to Niki and Pinky Wawn flew her back to Kai Tak. To the best of my knowledge, this was the last flight made by any C-47 to or from Macau.

1. **Airport**
2. **Outer Harbour**
3. **Reservoir for Water Supply**
4. **Artillery Barracks**
5. **Guia Lighthouse**

6. **Observatory**
7. **Government Hospital**
8. **Club of the Veterans of Great War I**
9. **St. Francisco Barracks**
10. **Ferreira do Amaral Monument**

Emperor Bao Dai with a senior-ranking French officer.

CHAPTER 4 : RESCUING AN EMPEROR — *In which my knowledge of French is found lacking, though my imagination fires on all cylinders.*

Bao Dai features on the cover of TIME.

On April 24, 1947, Betsy was grinding away the miles on the direct route from Bangkok to Hong Kong. Just ahead lay the beautiful sandy beaches of Vietnam and our navigation landmarks of the tiny Tonkin hamlets of Ron and Ba Don. The visibility was unlimited and a mosquito winking an eye at 100 miles was within the imagination. Yet, my body was impatiently restless. Was I coming down with the flu?

I sighed and recorded the time we crossed the coast in my navigation log. As I settled back, Alex Stewart, our radio officer, pushed a message into the skipper's hands and with a pixie grin said, "Pick the bones out of that." Captain Dick Hunt passed the message to me, disengaged George (the autopilot) and smoothly rolled the aircraft to starboard. "We'll just follow the coast," he said.

The message was a company directive to land at Tourane (now Danang) and await further instructions. Our track passed over Hue, the Imperial City, where the then-reigning Emperor of Annam was born in 1913. Tourane is a major port in Vietnam that spawns heavy cumulus clouds that sneak in from the South China Sea and lurk to ambush the unwary aviator. We survived many a terrifying 45 seconds negotiating those lightning-ridden formations and in that area we became acquainted with the descriptive name the American radar operators gave them – "snappers".

I had the impression that our skipper expected this message and was enjoying his little secret. Furthermore, we had offloaded a full load of freight at Bangkok, hastily installed seats, and flight-planned an empty plane to Hong Kong. That unusual procedure should have warned me that something was amiss. The plot thickened when our landing at

A quick turnaround for
a CX charter, 1946.

Tourane was free of the hassles that usually accompanied the French-controlled airfields.

An official, who was actually smiling, passed us through immigration and customs, and within minutes we were travelling along tree-lined boulevards in a spotlessly clean Citroen.

Dick was in his element. He jabbered in fluent French that thoroughly enthralled both him and our minder, yet not a word of explanation came our way. Finally, Alex and I began to jabber away in overbearing English that brought a look of injured reproach from our leader.

Our car screeched to a stop outside a large stone building guarded by mean-looking coppers who, recognising our minder, waved us through massive wooden gates. We were conducted to sleeping quarters that, though spartan, were bright and gave the impression that at least we were not Enemies of the State. I developed a twitch, though, when a high-ranking policeman with the beetling brows of the habitual criminal advised I should sleep with the window locked. With technicolor gore, he related how the Viet Minh lobbed nail and fishhook grenades through those windows using the trees that were an integral part of every boulevard. He then followed this with the unnecessary information that astute residents selected accommodation facing the parade-ground quadrangle; vital information yet worthless, for all such rooms were permanently occupied.

Vietnamese river transport.

Over supper, our skipper told us what it was all about. He did this in beautiful French, complete with hand gestures that got in a few additional meanings. Alex, in a moment of sheer bravado, reminded him that we did not understand the lingo. Our skipper gazed at him as a shoe gazes at a cockroach, raised his eyes heavenwards, and grudgingly repeated his manifesto in the language of the minions.

We were to fly out the Emperor Bao Dai and his entourage at first light. Until then we were confined to barracks. In spite of an increase in muscular pains and a headache, I protested violently, causing my skipper's grin to merely broaden.

It was a night best forgotten. In a pool of sweat, I rolled from side to side and I recall hearing regular explosions and small-arms fire creeping ever closer. Ho Chi Minh's communists ruled throughout the hours of darkness.

Emperor Bao Dai accepts due homage from his subjects.

On the way to Hong Kong, I kept mainly to the flight deck, but on a visit to the toilet I glimpsed two frothily dressed French girls. The Emperor Bao Dai had impeccable taste – they would have stopped traffic even on the Champs-Élysées. And yet I knew little of our royal passenger.

His father, Emperor Khai Dinh, took a concubine of peasant ancestry who gave birth to Nguyen Vinth Thuy on October 22, 1913. He received his education in France and hardly knew his homeland, but when he assumed the throne following the death of his father in 1926, he took the title Keeper of Greatness – or Bao Dai.

The Japanese entered Tonkin in late 1940 and by 1941 had subdued Indochina but allowed the Vichy government to hold nominal power until their coup de force in March 1945. This action led to the internment of all Frenchmen in Indochina. Against their better judgment, the Japanese allowed Bao Dai to remain as head of state but gave him no power. His regime collapsed when Japan surrendered in August 1945. The astute Ho Chi Minh grasped the opportunity and proclaimed the Democratic Republic of Vietnam with his capital in Hanoi. Ho's Viet Minh saw Bao Dai's symbolic value and asked him to stay as adviser. When Bao Dai realised he had no worthwhile role, he approached the French (whom he distrusted) to arrange his departure. Cathay Pacific accepted the charter and here we were, with the Playboy Emperor sprawled out in a starboard seat of Betsy's forward cabin. Our rescue mission remained a hush-hush operation that somehow escaped the ears of the media.

Bao Dai died in exile in Paris in July, 1997.

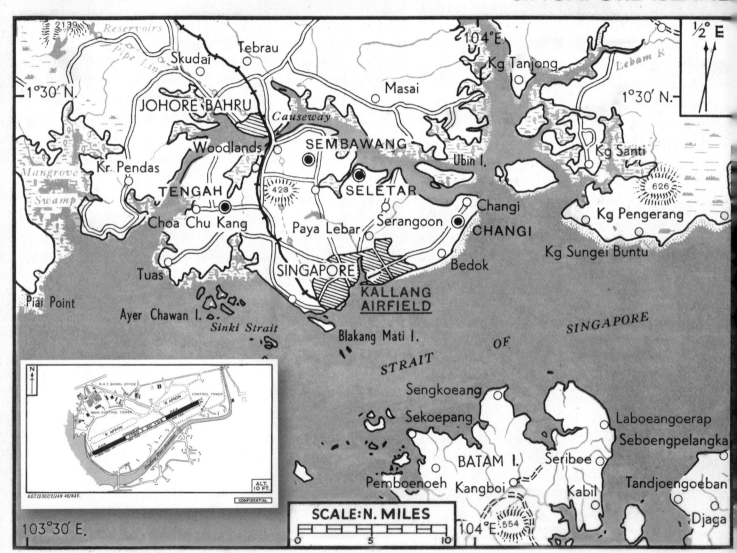

KALLANG
SINGAPORE ISLAND

01°18′N.
103°53′E.

ALT. 10 FT.
A.M.S.L.

½° E

2139
Reservoirs
Pipe Line

Skudai
Tebrau

1°30′N.
JOHORE BAHRU
Causeway
104°E
Kg Tanjong
Masai
1°30′N.
Lebam R

Woodlands
SEMBAWANG
Ubin I.
Kg Santi

Kr Pendas
423
SELETAR
626
Kg Pengerang

Mangrove
TENGAH
Changi

Swamp
Choa Chu Kang
Paya Lebar
Serangoon
CHANGI
Kg Sungei Buntu

Tuas
SINGAPORE
Bedok

Piai Point
KALLANG AIRFIELD
SINGAPORE

Ayer Chawan I.
Blakang Mati I.
STRAIT
OF
Sinki Strait

R.A.F. SIGNAL OFFICE
Control Tower
A. APRON
MAIN CONTROL TOWER
B. APRON

Sengkoeang
Sekoepang
Laboeangoerap
Seboengpelangka

ALT. 10 FT.
CONFIDENTIAL

BATAM I.
Seriboe
Tandjoengoeban

A.O.T.O/307/2/JAN 46/NAV.

SCALE: N. MILES
0   5   10

Pemboenoeh
Kangboi
Kabil
554
104°E
Djaga

103°30′E.

CHAPTER 5 : RUNNING THE DUTCH BLOCKADE — *In which Betsy engages in some not altogether official business*

Cathay Pacific lent its assistance to another regional conflict by accepting a charter from Dr. Sukarno's Indonesian Republic. This administration, established by the Japanese, had proclaimed Indonesian Independence at the end of the war. Unfortunately, the Dutch would not recognise its aspirations and blockades were in force around the republic's centres of power.

In mid-March 1947, the first of two charters, each of three weeks' duration, began. Betsy would handle the first charter and VR-HDJ (another Cathay C-47) the second. The agreement between Sukarno and Cathay Pacific was that the republic would purchase VR-HDJ when her charter period ended. Throughout the agreement, the republicans loosely referred to Betsy, and VR-HDJ, as Indonesian Republic One or IR-1.

Captains Vic Leslie and Dick Hunt and sparks Mum Louttit and K.K. Wong would rotate as crew. A Cathay Pacific junior pilot, Roy Hazelhurst, volunteered as first officer for the whole of this dangerous venture.

Radio Officer K.K. Wong tells these vivid memories of the operation:

"The charter was to run the Dutch air blockade mounted against Dr. Ahmed Sukarno's new Republic of Indonesia. Capt. Vic Leslie, F/O Roy Hazelhurst and I arrived at Singapore ready to go as soon as a few minor details were clarified. That evening, we dined at Raffles Hotel without the slightest idea of what we were required to do. Cathay Pacific was being canny! The dining room was bedlam and I kept intercepting glowering stares that were quickly averted as I made eye contact. The room was a motley collection of shady characters – the dregs of several nations.

CPA's VR-HDW glistens in the Singapore heat, with the Kallang Airport control tower in the background.

Capt. Vic Leslie, the co-commander of Betsy's dangerous Indonesian charter flights.

"Suddenly, two evil-looking Indonesians oiled their way to our table and raised our worst fears by croaking that the room was full of spies. They told us where we were going the next day. Apparently, everyone knew our objective but us! A little later, the information imparted by these seedy characters was confirmed by an official company memo.

"First light found us winging our way towards the island of Java and Sukarno's headquarters at Djokjakarta (Yogyakarta). From there we would fly to the island of Sumatra and land at Bukittinggi, a summer hill resort on its western side.

"I didn't know much about Djokjakarta, yet recalled a few details about Bukittinggi. In this fateful city, the revolutionary Sukarno collaborated with the Japanese occupation force through Colonel Fujiyama. The colonel, Commandant of Sumatra, occupied the mansion of a wealthy Dutchman that perched atop Lembah Ngarai with a ribbon of river meandering far below that emphasised those heights. The scenery was awesome.

"The three-week tour was strenuous for we made the return trip every day. With the oppressive heat and the nervous strain of routing close to the Dutch strongholds of Bandung and Batavia (now Jakarta), each trip left me thoroughly wrung out.

"My responsibility was communications. I had to maintain a continuous listening watch of all the signals crackling through the airwaves. Yet, for obvious reasons, I kept strict radio silence. The atmosphere was never free of static, yet it was vital I copy every signal sent by Changi, Singapore. I never learned how the company managed to get the co-operation of that RAF base, especially as the Dutch were not our enemies. Anyway, we had no interceptions and had not a single fright during the two tours I did; but I felt let down. For the whole period of my absence, nobody had bothered to tell my family anything of my movements – hardly the way to engender esprit de corps."

(K.K. Wong's qualifications were not recognised by the Hong Kong

Batavia
1287. Hoofd Postkantoor (Weltevreden)

licensing authority, and Cathay had to let the unlicensed Wong go. This licensing confusion between aeronautical countries exists to this day. Paradoxically, the very authority that had refused to support his qualifications quickly hired him. K.K. joined the Department of Civil Aviation in July 1947 as an air-traffic controller, and retired in October 1972.)

Transfer of VR-HDJ, as part of the charter arrangements, never took place, since the Indonesian Republic could not find the funds, and the Singapore Government impounded both plane and crew for operating illegally.

On May 3, 1947, concerned general manager Harry de Leuil convinced Max Oxford of the Hong Kong DCA of his company's innocence. Through his department, Oxford advised the Singapore authorities that the plane remained an asset of Cathay. That satisfied Singapore, who immediately released the detainees after several days of detention.

EPILOGUE

Behind the scenes at Djokjakarta, Roy Hazelhurst had curried favour with the aspiring aviation people in Sukarno's regime. When the Singapore authorities seized VR-HDJ, they loosened the purse strings, bought a C-47 from another source and employed Roy as her commander.

In addition to flying, he was also to prepare their flag-carrying airline for the moment the world recognised the new regime. At about the same time, a pilot named Cunningham was appointed to organise their anticipated Air Force. Meanwhile, they would fly the Djokjakarta /Bukittinggi milk run (daily routing) as co-captains.

On July 21, 1947, two Dutch Mustang fighters (some say they were P-40 Kitty Hawks) based at Batavia's (Jakarta's) Kemajoran airfield thundered into the air. Within minutes, they had intercepted the lumbering cargo plane, and blasted it into oblivion. There was one survivor, a passenger named Handokotjokro.

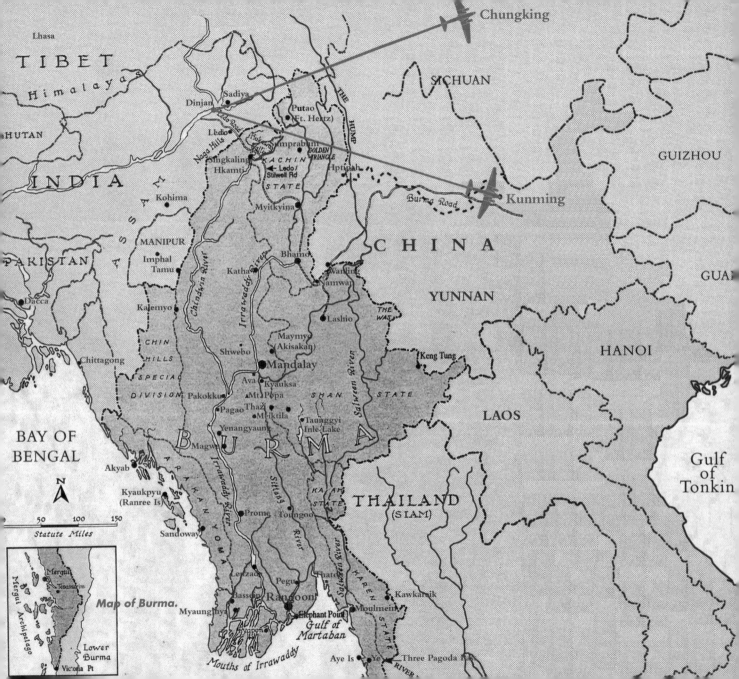

Map of Burma.

CHAPTER 6 : BURMESE DAYS — *Betsy flies into trouble and Kipling is taken to task*

The Union of Burma was born on January 4, 1948. The new government, however, had erred by not including the hill-country Karens, to the east and north, in its plans.

The commander-in-chief of the army at the time was Lieutenant General Smith Dun, a Karen and a first-class soldier. Other Karens held high rank in the government. They were far-sighted men who believed in Burma's unity and were determined that the Union would succeed.

Throughout 1948, the communist elements were the chief fomenters of trouble. Well-armed hooligan bands roved the country pillaging and raping, but they were unco-ordinated and more of an annoyance than a threat. But one fatal night, a masked gang rolled several hand grenades into Moulmein's Roman Catholic church. The carnage was ghastly. Moulmein was at the time hosting a battalion of Karen infantry. They had reached the end of their tether and a vicious civil war began against their traditional Burman enemies, whom they blamed for the atrocity.

January 31, 1949 is regarded as the date when the Karen insurgency began in earnest. Soon, the Karen forces controlled the railways, roads and rivers. With Rangoon under siege, its airport of Mingaladon became the hub that supplied food for the country's survival. This situation heralded a flood of other aircraft-charter companies. Most were earnest operators, others were blackguards and villains.

Cathay Pacific's association with Burma had predated this organised Karen rebellion by about a year, and the sporadic trouble caused by the communists had brought plenty of work. However, the insurgency increased that work tenfold. Cathay personnel were posted to Burma for tours of several weeks and accommodated in a spartan mess on University Avenue.

Ken Begg (left) and Vic Leslie relaxing at Cathay's University Road Mess, Rangoon, Burma, 1948.

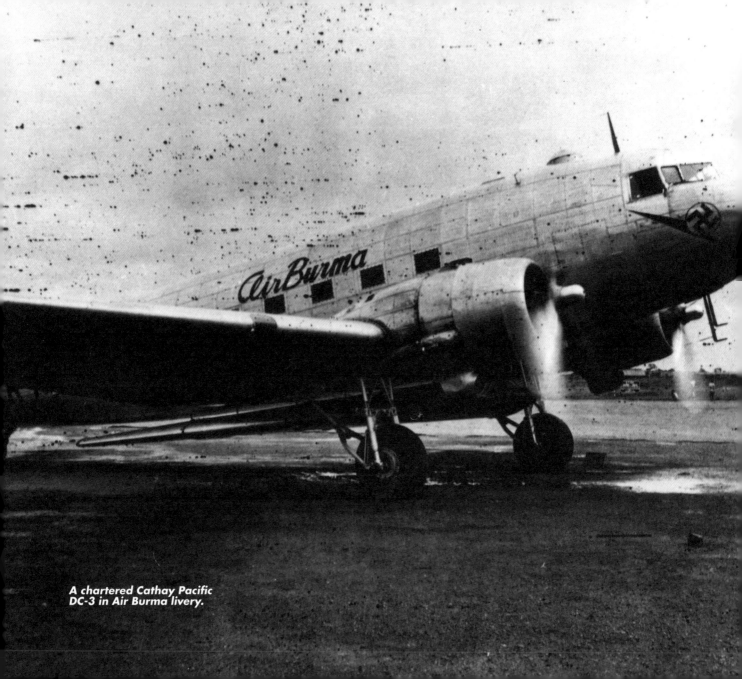

A chartered Cathay Pacific DC-3 in Air Burma livery.

Without Mingaladon and the charter operators, it is likely the Karen insurgency would have succeeded. One night, the Karens overran the area and then, without reason, retired after inflicting only superficial damage [see Chapter 7]. A few well-laid charges of explosives would have destroyed the Burmese Air Force installation and also the charter planes. One of these was Cathay's Betsy, which had returned with an engine failure just before dusk.

The story begins in September 1948 in Meiktila, central Burma. In command of Betsy was Captain Carlton Fletcher "Pat" Moore, and I was his first officer. Our charter was to rush Burmese troops to Moulmein to support troops defending the airfield there. As the men in full battle gear boarded, I saw Pat lying under the tail casually puffing his disgusting pipe. His eyes were riveted on the tail wheel strut. Suddenly he shouted, "Stop!" and ordered the last two soldiers to leave the plane. They left with ill grace, but Pat's action had undoubtedly lengthened their life spans.

Betsy left Meiktila with 57 soldiers and a crew of two. After departure, I asked him why he had been under the tail. His voice, booming through a cloud of noxious smoke, told me he had learned that trick when he was flying for Indian operators – the undisputed masters of overloading aircraft. By watching the tail strut shorten, one could determine the maximum take-off weight without actually weighing each item. So, here was the crafty Pat, who had invented most of aviation's shortcuts, benefiting from another's devious methods. That canny old wolf taught me a lot!

Pat slammed us down on the perimeter of Moulmein Airfield with bullets peppering the area. A major battle was in progress. Our courageous troops deplaned without waiting for the port engine to wind down, and charged to engage the enemy. While Betsy was shuttering to a stop, he yelled, "Don't let anyone pin the undercarriage." With bullets pinging all around me, I zealously guarded those wheels. Pat's

**FLYING is the way to travel
– and CPA the way to FLY.**

BANGKOK
Leaving Tuesday, 4th March .... Fare $528.
SINGAPORE
Leaving Tuesday, 4th March .... Fare $880.
MANILA
Leaving Tuesday, 11th March .... Fare $600.
SYDNEY
Leaving Tuesday, 11th March .... Fare $2,200.

Passenger & Freight Booking Agents
**(P. J. LOBO & CO.)
4 CHATER ROAD**
TEL: 31162 & 31400
Kowloon Office: Tel. 58081 Extn. 8

Cathay Pacific
AIRWAYS

Cathay Pacific was quick to claim its position as Hong Kong's premier airline.

The collective living conditions of the wonderful dwellers at Number 156 Irrawaddy Delta, Burma has an ageless simplicity totally devoid of the amenities of their city cousins.

scream of "Let's get the hell out of here!" galvanised me into action – with three strides and a herculean leap, I was aboard and slamming the rear door. On hands and knees, I grovelled up the aisle, fighting the acceleration, and plonked into my seat just as we clipped the top branches of the perimeter trees. As Pat skidded Betsy around the famous Moulmein Pagoda, he ordered wheels up. To my horror, they wouldn't budge. Pat's reproachful look deflated me more than any words of anger could have achieved.

We flew back to Mingaladon with wheels extended, fervently hoping the engines would not lose a beat. Our walk-around disclosed not a single bullet hole – unbelievable luck. Then up rushed my skipper, brandishing the undercarriage pins he had removed, and his hand squeezed my shoulder – they were clearly marked "Moulmein", that station's stand-by pins. That squeeze increased my miserable height by at least a yard! In the split second from leaving my post until Pat poured on the power, someone had pinned the wheels. It took real guts to remember standing instructions with a battle raging. Perhaps this was taking good training a little too far!

Soon after, the Rangoon manager handed Pat a note. Our brave soldiers had been killed to a man within 15 minutes of our departure, but their sacrifice had kept Moulmein Airfield safely in government hands.

We began approaching most charters in a mood of casual expectancy. Occasionally, however, a straightforward charter would take an unexpected and almost bizarre twist.

Bob "Smithy" Smith recalls this trip with Betsy from October 1948:

"One glorious Sunday morning, I arrived at the Kokine Swimming Club to while away the day admiring the Creator's other creations. I felt this was the way every day should be, but a fickle fate enjoys interfering with a man's recreational plans. Suddenly, a shadow darkened the sun that proved to be the ample form of the club manager. He told me Captain John Paish was on the phone. John's flight engineer had reported sick and would I take his place for a short charter to Toungoo (Toungoo is about 120 miles north of Rangoon on the Sittang River and was once the home of the legendary AVG – the Flying Tigers). I returned to the pool and told them I would be back for a late lunch. Eric Aylward, who was looking bored, asked if he could come along for the ride. My ready agreement proved another of my many mistakes!

An aerial view of Moulmein. The Moulmein Pagoda can be seen in the upper right of the photo.

"We arrived at Mingaladon to find the cargo securely tied down and covered by an old tarpaulin. Three villainous-looking soldiers were sprawled along the top. John Paish waved away the soldiers to do his mandatory check. Suddenly, he froze by the unmistakable cocking of automatic weapons. In a stage whisper, he told us to back off. We returned to the dispatch office and told the co-ordinating Burmese officer that unless he withdrew his men so a check could be made, the cargo could sit there and rot.

Betsy, wearing her VR-HDB registration, flying over western Hong Kong Island in 1947.

"The officer got belligerent but Paish was unmoved. A telephone call to his superior calmed him down. With ill-concealed disgust, he ordered his men out of the plane and we began our check. We found not the manifested foodstuffs but sweating gelignite of pre-war vintage. Age does this to gelignite and makes it dangerously unstable to the point where a gentle bump can set it off. To add to the problem, a box of detonators lay on top of the tarpaulin with three Sten guns propped against the box. Each gun had a bullet in the spout. A ladylike sneeze could set those guns off.

"We managed to take the box of detonators to the rear of the plane. I told Paish that I would not fly unless the guns were unloaded. As I spoke, Eric Aylward kept nodding profusely. Paish told the officer of our democratic decision but he refused to order the weapons unloaded."

Eric Aylward takes up the story:

"Smithy suddenly raced over to Moultrie's Palace of Germs [see Chapter 7] and returned with a dozen bottles of beer. While the guards were glugging away, he removed the live clips and replaced them with empty ones. At Toungoo, we learned the gelignite was to blow the Sittang bridges in the face of a rebel advance. I reckon there was more danger to the handlers than the bridges."

Heading home, John Paish flew most of the way below 100 feet. He had a great respect for

Mingaladon Airport,
Rangoon, June 1949.

the Swiss Oerlikon guns the rebels operated with such expertise. It was interesting to see the rebels flinging themselves into the muddy paddy fields as they screeched past but their hearts did not share in the rebels' discomfort.

Fifty miles from Mingaladon, John Paish climbed to a comfortable 5,000 feet. Then, without preamble, Smithy declared, "Rudyard Kipling is wrong!" The others had no idea what he was on about, but seeing he had their full attention, he argued that, "If the pagoda faced eastward it would face into China and consequently couldn't possibly face the sea." (See the poem Mandalay by Rudyard Kipling.)

Thus began a heated discussion between Smithy and Eric that finally gave John the Jimmy-Brits. He decided to settle the matter by diverting to Moulmein just to get a little peace. They crossed the Gulf of Martaban and landed at Moulmein where Smithy was proven right – Kipling had erred. Smithy was so pleased he bought them a curry lunch at a little native eatery just below the pagoda. The meal was first-class, but when they tried to start, there was not a peep from Betsy's starboard engine. An inspection found that a bullet had sheared the connecting drive of the starter.

They received a replacement starter at first light the next morning, and some time later Syd de Kantzow tackled Eric Aylward. "You were on that flight. Tell me, how did you get

so far off course? Surely you could see the Rangoon Shwe Dagon Shrine glittering in the sun?" When Eric disclosed the whole story, Syd scowled. "Are you saying you grounded a plane for 24 hours and used hundreds of gallons of fuel just to prove Kipling's statement? I know who started that argument – it was that bloody stirrer Smithy, wasn't it?"

Picture-postcard views of Burma.

16° 54′ N.
96° 08′ E.

ELEV. **100** FT.

A.M.S.L.

G. 1. 130.
MINGALADON
BURMA

1° W

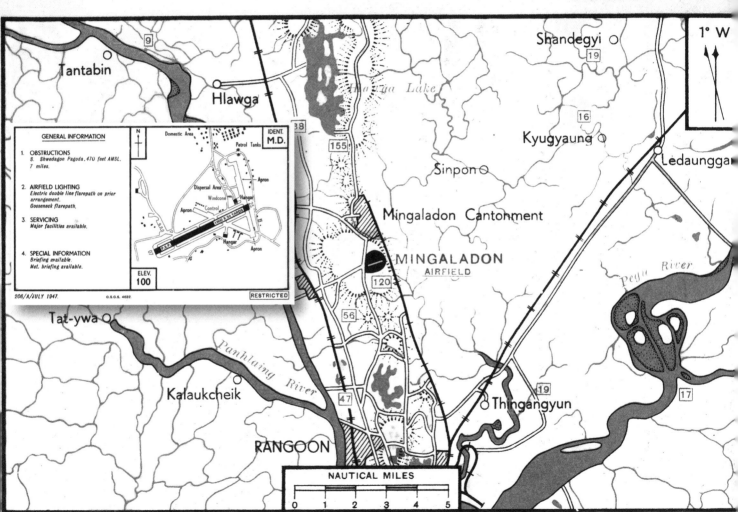

GENERAL INFORMATION

1. **OBSTRUCTIONS**
   S. Shwedagon Pagoda, 470 feet AMSL.
   7 miles.

2. **AIRFIELD LIGHTING**
   Electric double line flarepath on prior
   arrangement.
   Gooseneck flarepath.

3. **SERVICING**
   Major facilities available.

4. **SPECIAL INFORMATION**
   Briefing available.
   Met. briefing available.

IDENT.
M.D.

Domestic Area

Petrol Tanks

Apron

Dispersal Area

Windcone   Hangar

Apron   Control

Hangar   Apron

ELEV.
100

RESTRICTED

206/A/JULY 1947.   G.S.G.S. 4632

Tantabin

Hlawga

Shandegyi

19

16

Kyugyaung

Ledaungga

Sinpon

Mingaladon Cantonment

MINGALADON
AIRFIELD

Pegu River

Tat-ywa

Kalaukcheik

Panhlaing River

RANGOON

Thingangyun

19

17

NAUTICAL MILES

0   1   2   3   4   5

ALL HEIGHTS IN FEET ABOVE MEAN SEA LEVEL

CHAPTER 7 : FIREWORKS AT MINGALADON — *In which Betsy has a narrow escape and it's a free-for-all at the Palace of Germs*

***Burmese Air Force
Air Marshall Tommie Clift (left)
and General Ne Win.***

Ground engineers are my favourite people. They are astonishingly versatile and take in their stride the most unlikely situations. If the situation is interestingly unique, it spurs them to greater effort. Their avowed aim is to outsmart any mechanical mischief that an aircraft can devise.

The day the Karens surrounded Mingaladon brought another nail-biting experience to Bob "Smithy" Smith, Cathay's resident ground engineer.

Smithy recalls:

"Earlier in the day, the Karens blocked the Prome Road. That meant we were stranded at Mingaladon. We did, however, get warning the Karens were advancing on the airport and managed to fly most of our aircraft and personnel to Bangkok but one Cathay C-47 (Betsy) remained on the tarmac needing an engine change. That day, Johnnie Riordan had returned with a feathered prop. Checking found it had a failed master rod bearing. Eric Aylward, a guy named Jacobs, and a couple of others had stayed to help me work on it."

Despite an unearthly silence, they knew the Karens were biding their time and would soon overrun the field. This kept them interested in their work. Bob estimated the engine would be installed soon after dark. Then all they had to do was to replace the cowls, give it a quick run, get Riordan from the RAF Mission across the strip and take off for the fleshpots of Bangkok.

Smithy and Eric went across to the Palace of Germs [see sidebar] to bring back something to eat. The lights were on but there was no sign of Moutrie or his minions. They had scuttled off at the first smell of trouble. The tables, however, were loaded with food and – something

LOOSELY CALLED A RESTAURANT,
The Palace of Germs was run by a dried-
out Anglo-Burman, whom we called Old-
man Moutrie. Hygiene was an unknown
concept to him and cockroaches held sway
after lights-out. One reliable authority
claimed the roaches answered to specific
names, while another assured me that the
understanding owner had issued them with
identity passes to assure them freedom of
movement.

Moutrie concocted a curry that was
the nectar of the gods. Its aroma and taste
belied its dangers for it could penetrate
granite and, furthermore, it had the unique
capability of producing two different
strains of diarrhoea from the one serving.
That curry was the bane of American
ground engineer George Stephenson's
existence. This gentle giant would answer
to Big George or The Farmer, and in fact
took no umbrage at what one called him,
providing it was not too late for nosh. Big
George had an appetite proportional to his
massive bulk. He knew he would suffer
after a Moutrie curry and yet he devoured
it with a disgusting enthusiasm, accepting
the resulting fait accompli.

that brought a thoughtful gleam to Eric's face – the bar had been left
wide open. Accepting this largesse, Smithy crammed a large cardboard
box with food. With slightly different priorities, Eric filled two massive
crushed-ice buckets with grog and Smithy's group had a banquet beneath
Betsy's wing. Before long, nobody gave a damn if the Karens came, or in
what numbers.

They finished the engine in the dark using cardboard tubes to restrict
the light of their torches. Their progress was good until a barrage of
shells whined overhead and exploded behind the Burmese Air Force
hangar. The Karen artillery repeated their barrage every ten minutes,
but between each barrage racing hands were getting the job done. When
a star shell turned the night to day, Smithy's mob decided that enough
was enough. They scuttled into the paddy fields across the runway, and
there between the waving stalks of rice they had a front-row view of the
bombardment.

Eric wanted them to sneak back and fly Betsy away. He didn't care
about her lack of cowls or a run-up – he just wanted to get out. Smithy
asked who would fly it, and Eric sneered: "Smithy, you keep telling us
you hold a flying licence, so fly the bloody thing."

Smithy was a fine pilot who had trained with me at the Mascot Royal
Aero Club, but he hadn't handled anything as big as a C-47 and sensibly
refused to take the bait.

Just before dawn, a platoon of Karens politely knocked at the door of
the BAF hangar. Suddenly, figures were seen jumping from windows and
dashing across the runway, achieving the difficult feat of changing from
uniforms into mufti on the run.

The Karens screamed with glee at their antics, and with the last man
dwindling into the distance they smashed the controls and bayoneted the
fuel tanks of the Airspeed Oxfords and the Spitfire.

Smithy later said: "It surprised us when the Karens didn't burn the
BAF aircraft. Later, they took part in the final defeat of the rebels. The

VHF radio sets were all they removed. They used these to good advantage by establishing a good communication network at their Toungoo headquarters. When one considers the extent of the shelling, there was very little damage. It flattened the International Aeradio premises and added a few more shrapnel scars to the BAF hangar.

"The Aeradio fellows were a good bunch and did not deserve to lose everything. What a blessing if the shells had erred just a few yards. They would have eliminated the Palace of Germs – a blessing to everyone!"

The Control Tower at Mingaladon Airfield, 1947.

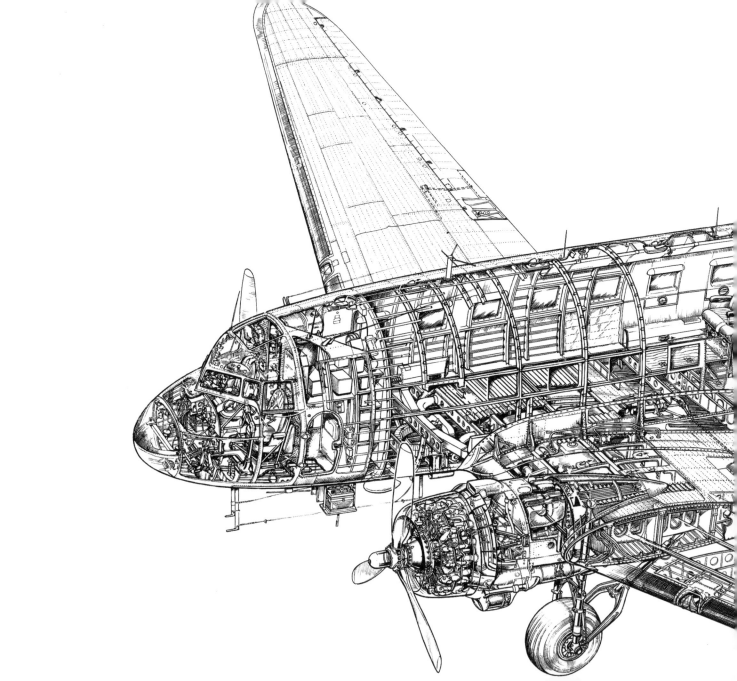

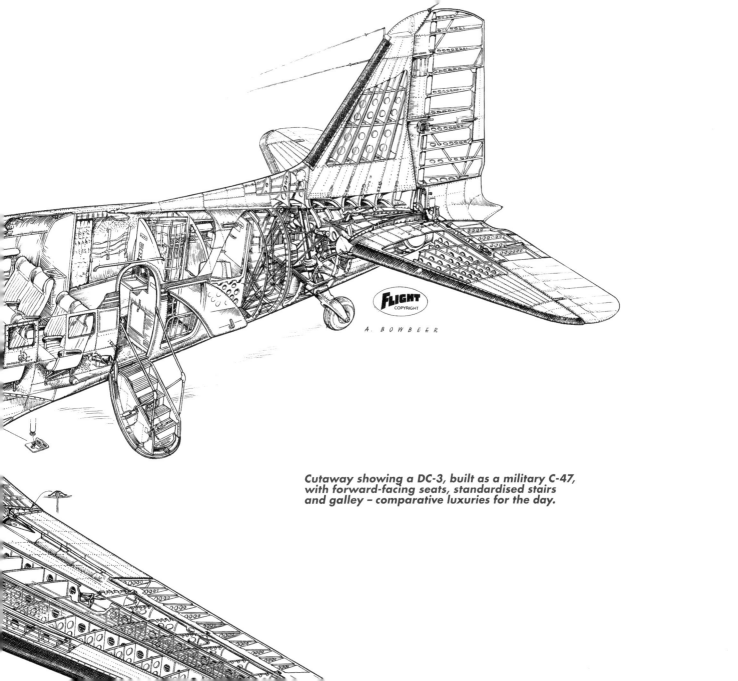

FLIGHT
COPYRIGHT

A. BOWBEER

Cutaway showing a DC-3, built as a military C-47, with forward-facing seats, standardised stairs and galley – comparative luxuries for the day.

Betsy at Anisakan Airfield, Burma, 1948.

CHAPTER 8 : THE CAPTURE OF MAYMYO — *In which the issue of danger money is resolved with some help from Betsy*

Although the Karens held most of the countryside, several large cities and towns – although surrounded – continued to resist. We began supplying them with the necessities of life, never sure when we departed Mingaladon if these cities remained in friendly hands or otherwise. Consequently, a series of coloured sheets were displayed near the windsock of landing areas to indicate whether or not it was safe to land. These were changed daily and our pre-departure briefing included this vital information.

Many aircraft were returning to Mingaladon with bullet holes in their wings and fuselage. The situation for the civilian charter operators was causing concern, for we were in a vicious shooting war. In a moment of lighthearted banter, the Cathay crew devised a lottery. The plane with the most bullet holes won a case of beer. Unfortunately, a devious element cheated the system by placing patches over non-existent bullet holes. This betrayal of trust forced our lottery into liquidation.

The situation worsened dramatically when the Karens captured the major railway terminal at Insein. This put them within a couple of miles of Mingaladon and within mortar range of the end of the main runway. A few eagle-eyed snipers began to fire on anything that moved near the runway and a couple of bends in the road ran between our mess and the airport. Worse, we were forced to use the abandoned RAF runway that was basically unserviceable. It was rough and potted, particularly at the ends, and consequently our take-off load was seriously reduced.

Neither our pay nor insurance cover was adjusted to compensate for these hairy conditions. When a crew member broached the subject, he found himself faced with stony silence or derision.

VIP transport in rural Burma.

January 5, 1950. Cathay Pacific Airways launches a service to Sandakan. Captain Phil Blown (in centre) surrounded by the Dayak Chief and his retinue. Behind Phil is R/O John 'Fitz' Fitzgerald with Syd de Kantzow (at far right).

One afternoon, we met in Bob Smith's hole-in-the-wall office at the rear of the main hangar. The agenda was to compose a letter to the management, expressing our concern that the Burma operation had reached excessively dangerous levels. Without warning, a 20mm Oerlikon shell pushed its snout through the wall. All present held their breath, and almost instantly, everyone cleared not only the office but the hangar as well. After a time, we decided our letter was vital and returned to the menacing object. Bob Smith's casual one-finger typing reached subsonic speed and soon the letter was ready for signing. Shaking hands scribbled mostly illegible signatures, but who cared! That afternoon, Ceddie Carlton, the Angry Ant [see sidebar], took it back to Hong Kong.

On the morning of March 5, 1949, Captain Dick Hunt, our operations manager, arrived at Mingaladon to fly Betsy up to Meiktila with Captain John Riordan. What better way to show his contempt than to do a flight up-country? As he entered the flight deck, he ordered Riordan to "hop into the right hand seat". And off they went.

As the flight continued, so did the lecturing along the lines of "how bloody frightened you blokes have become, using every pretence to squeeze more money off a struggling impoverished company". His soulful plea brought a tear to Riordan's eyes, but retribution lay just ahead.

At Meiktila, the airfield signal was correct, indicating that it was in government hands. As he cut the engines, Hunt said, "Look John! Must be a VIP coming back with us. We've got a guard of honour." John looked and wryly remarked, "Yes! We have, and they look like Karens."

"Bloody rot," scoffed Hunt.

Riordan merely shrugged, then walked back to open the cargo door. As he pushed it open, he got a precise salute from a diminutive officer whose serious expression spread to a wide grin as he said, "I'm Captain New Seng, a Karen."

"I expected nothing less," replied Riordan, returning the salute. Then he excused himself and returned to the flight deck to impart the good news. In a subdued whisper, Hunt asked what they should do. "Just what they bloody well tell us," the realistic Riordan advised.

The Karens locked the crew in a room. Later, a guard tapped on the door, and in plummy Oxford English asked if they had any special request for dinner. Hunt said he wasn't hungry but would appreciate a beer. John, testing what the traffic would bear, asked for a

THE 450 PAGOD

ONTAINING THE TABLES OF THE LAW
MANDALAY, BURMAH,

medium-rare steak and a woman for dessert. Neither request surprised the guard who soon returned with his required steak, a case of beer, and two women.

As the new dawn came up like thunder, the Karen captain awoke them personally with his orders for the day. He casually told them they were greatly honoured – for they were to help in the capture of Maymyo. They would fly his troops to the airfield of Anisakan, from where his men would capture Maymyo, some five miles away. They would take off immediately! "What if we refuse?" snarled Hunt. The still-smiling officer unholstered his revolver, blew down the barrel, in a manner pleasing to the Western movie buff, and quietly said, "Now, Captain, I fervently hope you are not going to be difficult?"

Maymyo is about 65 miles northwest of Meiktila and just east of the legendary city of Mandalay. The hill town of Maymyo became an oasis for a Raj community escaping the summer heat of the Irrawaddy delta, but they earned their cool holiday by surviving a narrow road of frightening bends. By 1949, the civilised traveller arrived at the pocket-sized airfield at Anisakan.

On March 7, 1949, Betsy, Hunt and Riordan flew two loads of Karen troops to Anisakan, and by the early evening Maymyo had fallen to the invaders. The casual way the Karens captured the airfield showed their superiority to the Burmans. A few minutes after they landed at

THE LATE CAPTAIN Cedric Carlton
was of small stature, weighing 100lb when
soaking wet. His temper beguiled his size;
he was argumentative and ever-restless. He
considered every red-blooded male had
the right of a good punch-up; yet he never
won a fight, although he never retreated
from a fray that he knew would ultimately
end in his demise. He was the archetypal
good mate and earned the nickname of the
Angry Ant. We all respected him.

More importantly, he possessed
abounding courage. On July 23, 1954, he
and Captain Phil Blown, a man of similar
courage, found themselves murderously
blasted out of the sky by Chinese fighter
planes just off the coast of Hainan Island.
As their Cathay Skymaster plummeted
towards the sea, they fought their mangled
plane until the moment of impact. Their
outstanding airmanship earned the Queen's
Commendation for Valuable Services in the
Air. They were decorated on June 15, 1955
by Hong Kong Governor Sir Alexander
Grantham.

Anisakan, they had full control of the airfield. A Karen squad, dressed in
government-army uniforms, mounted a guard in front of the huts that
gave service as a terminal facility.

A short time later, an Airspeed Oxford of the Burmese Air Force
touched down. The unsuspecting crew taxied in, cut the engines, and
were imprisoned. Under Karen persuasion, they revealed that a Spitfire
would soon land. Still in government uniforms, the Karens made things
look lazy and normal, and the Spitfire pilot joined his colleagues in the
brig.

The capture of the important hill town of Maymyo was little more
than a walk in the park. As the defenders saw the Karens flitting from
tree to tree, they realised their own inadequacies and fled into the jungle.

Hunt and Riordan made no further contribution to the Karen war
effort. For two days, the Karens treated them as honoured guests. They
were driven to Betsy to find her thoroughly cleaned and sparkling like a
new pin.

Then the diminutive captain autographed Riordan's logbook,
plucked off his artillery badge and pinned in on Riordan's jacket. He
removed Riordan's Cathay Pacific wings and pinned them to his tunic
as his men broke into spontaneous applause. Facing Riordan, he said,
"When we capture Rangoon we'll make you the first Marshall of the
Karen Air Force." With a serious demeanour, Riordan accepted the
accolade.

His words to Hunt were in stark contrast. "Captain, I don't like you,"
he said. "I am releasing you because your colleague asked it of me, but do
not fall into my hands again."

A thoroughly chastened Hunt hastened back to Hong Kong where he
reported that the Burma operation did entail a "certain amount of risk".
We all got a 50 per cent pay rise plus 30 rupees an hour danger money.

Wingaba Lakes,
Rangoon.

VR-HEN performed like a homing pigeon.

Cathay Pacific Plane Damaged By Ground Fire Near Rangoon

RANGOON, April 22—(AP) —A Cathay Pacific aircraft on a chartered flight over the delta yesterday was damaged by ground fire near the rice port of Bassein, 90 miles West of Rangoon, official sources reported.

The starboard engine was put out of commission, but the aircraft landed safely at Bassein and none of the passengers were injured.

CHAPTER 9 : NIKI SHOT DOWN — *In which Niki takes a bullet and her downfall proves to have been her salvation.*

An example of a Cathay Pacific pilot's logbook. This record of his flying experience follows every pilot throughout his career.

April 21, 1949 found Capt. John Riordan and me flying west from Mingaladon to the delta city of Bassein. Our roster scheduled three return flights for the day, but fate had its own agenda. We skipped along at tree-top level staying in contact with the ground, for Bassein had no radio aids, and our monsoon experience had taught us that this was the only way to handle that 70-mile flight. We occasionally diverted around a nasty squall, but the forward visibility remained reasonable.

As we crossed north of the strip, small-arms fire struck Niki. The starboard engine stopped and flames billowed past my sliding window. The flight deck filled with acrid smoke belching from the joins in the companionway. I grabbed a fire extinguisher and rushed into the cabin but there was no evidence of fire. As I re-entered the flight deck, our radio officer Bo Egan materialised like a smoky wraith. The skipper had ordered him to monitor the rear door for a forced landing.

Back in my seat, I found John losing the battle to restart the starboard engine. We were so low that I could see the blight on the tree leaves. The port engine was screaming under full power, however, and our airspeed was in the safe range. John screeched that he couldn't hold Niki much longer and would make a landing just ahead, but I had seen something that had escaped my skipper and I yelled, if he did, we'd all be killed. Great earthworks, broad enough to take a bullock cart, surrounded the paddy fields. "Let's try for the landing strip. I'll look after the engine and call the speeds," I yelled. He merely nodded.

The strip was appearing in and out of rain squalls to port but, with someone to handle the inside work, John kept the strip in sight. Our combined efforts worked out splendidly, and when he rolled the wheels onto that grassy haven our sighs of relief could be heard above the mud

CPA's DC-3s being prepared for take-off.

splashing our flame-scarred fuselage.

Strangely, after the initial flame and smoke, the fire seemed to be extinguished – later we learned the reason. Safe on the ground, Bo Egan radioed Mingaladon advising of our plight and requested a ground engineer. We felt our signal told the ground engineer everything, but actually it told him little. "Smithy" Smith, Cathay's station engineer, left within minutes in a Norseman flown by Paul Clevenger.

Paul terrified Smithy with his lack of experience on the Norseman, and even before the plane had come to a complete stop he had gathered all his equipment, jumped out and screeched at Paul: "Bugger off, I'll take my chances with the Karen rebels." Although not much of a pilot, Paul was no fool; seeing the flinty look in Smithy's eyes, he quickly swung his plane around and belted off down the strip.

Our message had told Smithy little more than that our starboard engine had stopped and the cockpit had filled with smoke. He thought that was a bit weird and not knowing what he should take had brought everything he could. It took him a while to solve the problem until he discovered a small hole in the leading edge of the wing. Getting on top of Niki's wing, he found a gaping hole where the bullet had exited. He opened an access panel and found that a bullet had gone through the centre of a fuel line so precisely that it had flared it and

consequently starved the starboard engine of fuel. Luckily, he had brought some hose and clamps. He cut the damaged hose two inches either side of the flared hole, bell-mouthed the ends, and then installed a piece of Hi-Pressure flex. It would get us back to Mingaladon where he could make a permanent repair. That very temporary repair remained in place for months. Later, when he lifted the flight deck floor, he found all the zinc chromate burnt a brown colour and the protective grease on the control cables a mass of blisters.

From the time we were shot down, the firing around the strip was sporadic. Now the firing had increased to where bullets screamed regularly overhead and it was clearly time to get Niki out.

While enjoying a celebratory drink at Green's Hotel later, Smithy said, "That's why your engine stopped. It was starved of fuel. The reason the fire went out was the rush of fuel prevented ignition, it actually smothered the flames."

Then he presented John with a trophy – that piece of pipe, now a sparkling copper hue, mounted on a polished teak base. In thanks, Riordan said, "It was IFR (Instrument Flying Rules) outside, then the flight deck filled with smoke and it became IFR inside."

True to the music halls of yesteryear, his audience roared, "So what did you do?"

To which he spontaneously replied, "We broke the instruments glass and finished the flight on Braille."

The applause brought down the house.

CPA's VR-HEN flying with Air Burma livery is readied to carry a new wing out to Betsy.

Bob "Smithy" Smith stands in front of the 'Wing-Sling' he has fitted to the belly of VR-HEN.

CHAPTER 10 : THE BHAMO FIASCO — *In which Betsy loses a wing and some careful calculations save the day.*

This incident happened on an up-country airstrip at Bhamo, near the Chinese border in upper Burma and close to the legendary Burma Road. It was June 5, 1949, the plane was Betsy, and the skipper was an experienced man, but the cause was pilot error brought about by a self-assured attitude.

Standing instructions state that, when a captain flies an aircraft without a first officer, he must start the starboard engine first. To fully observe the start, he must occupy the right-hand pilot seat, usually occupied by the first officer. When the engine is stabilised, he resumes his normal seat and starts the port engine. This procedure allowed a pilot to immediately handle any problem that may arise during the start sequence. The skipper ignored these procedures, and when a worried radio officer tried to draw his attention to an abnormality, he was told to keep his advice to himself until it was sought. The radio officer felt he had a genuine grievance since he was choking on the thick black smoke that suddenly invaded his radio alcove. This was a tiny work area just aft and to the right of his skipper's seat.

Humming away, the skipper taxied the merrily burning aircraft the full length of the runway. He turned into the wind and presumably made the mandatory magneto checks. Just as he applied take-off power, the starboard engine fell off.

Eric Aylward drew the short straw and was sent to Bhamo to analyse the situation. Being an astute man, he initially discussed his options with Smithy. The major problem was getting a replacement wing to Bhamo. It must go by air for all surface transport was at a standstill. Then,

The serviceable wing from a written-off Thai C-47 is prepared for transportation.

VR-HEN *fires up her engines prior to take-off with the under-slung wing.*

The wing being fitted to VR-HEN

Betsy in trouble. A close-up of
the damaged starboard engine.

having got it there, where would they find the installation equipment? The burnt-out engine presented no problem, for a new engine could go by ferry plane. The engine support nacelle was twisted beyond repair. This meant Eric must choose a replacement from Cathay Pacific's Manila aircraft dump.

At Mingaladon, there was a serviceable wing attached to a written-off C-47 (Pete Holmes had lost hydraulic pressure and ground-looped her). This C-47 carried the Siamese registration HS-TA180 and Trans-Asiatic Airlines (TAAS) owned her. Captain Dallas Cederberg directed the fortunes of Trans-Asiatic.

Naturally, the lost earning power of a C-47 disturbed Cathay and they badgered Eric to get it ready by yesterday. The method devised to transport the wing by Eric and Smithy brought them fame in the aviation industry. One authority generously compared it to Sol Soldinsky's famous DC-2½ [see sidebar]. Throughout the operation, Ted Amor, chief technical officer with Burma's Department of Civil Aviation, haunted the joint.

The Anisakan airstrip facilities as seen from Betsy's cockpit.

The scheme was to jack up the Cederberg wreck and with enough clearance they devised a sling and brackets. It was here that Smithy showed his world-class welding ability. They transferred the sling to VR-HEN, a Cathay C-47, and stowed the replacement wing. Everything was go! Eric takes up the story:

"We were about to leave when Ted Amor arrived in a flurry of indignant rage. He demanded to know our Centre of Gravity. When I said I hadn't a clue, he nearly had a cardiac arrest. Short of breath, he gasped that we couldn't take off until we had found it.

"Smithy, who is a wizard with figures, including those numerical, grabbed the form. He quickly calculated a value that completely mystified everyone. Ted peered at it in disbelief, then grudgingly agreed that Smithy indeed had found the elusive Centre of Gravity (four inches in front of the desired range centre). The flight to Bhamo was incident-free.

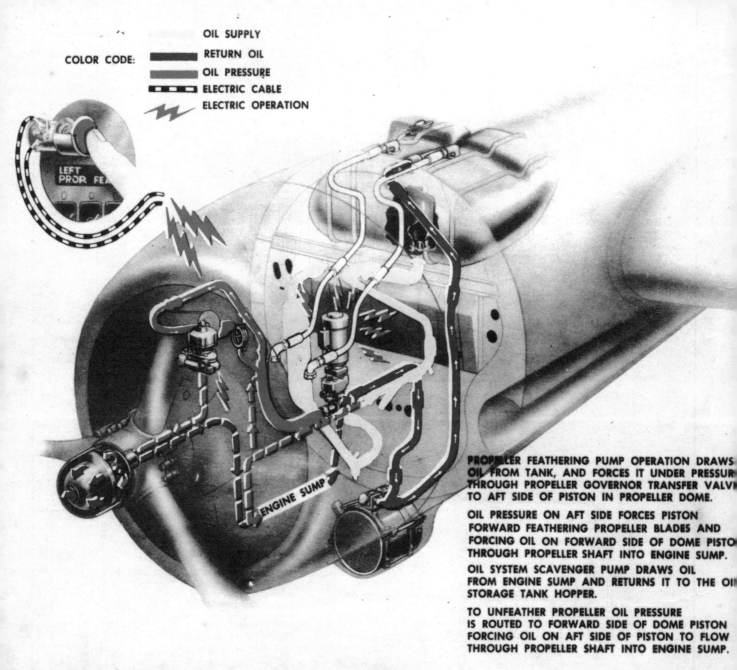

COLOR CODE:
- OIL SUPPLY
- RETURN OIL
- OIL PRESSURE
- ELECTRIC CABLE
- ELECTRIC OPERATION

LEFT PROP FEA

ENGINE SUMP

PROPELLER FEATHERING PUMP OPERATION DRAWS OIL FROM TANK, AND FORCES IT UNDER PRESSURE THROUGH PROPELLER GOVERNOR TRANSFER VALVE TO AFT SIDE OF PISTON IN PROPELLER DOME.

OIL PRESSURE ON AFT SIDE FORCES PISTON FORWARD FEATHERING PROPELLER BLADES AND FORCING OIL ON FORWARD SIDE OF DOME PISTON THROUGH PROPELLER SHAFT INTO ENGINE SUMP.

OIL SYSTEM SCAVENGER PUMP DRAWS OIL FROM ENGINE SUMP AND RETURNS IT TO THE OIL STORAGE TANK HOPPER.

TO UNFEATHER PROPELLER OIL PRESSURE IS ROUTED TO FORWARD SIDE OF DOME PISTON FORCING OIL ON AFT SIDE OF PISTON TO FLOW THROUGH PROPELLER SHAFT INTO ENGINE SUMP.

"Our pilot, Captain Jimmy Harper of Douglas, found the additional drag was negligible. I think we lost about seven knots and needed a little more elevator trim than usual. There was no crane at Bhamo, but they did have a thirty-ton gantry. It had the power to lift a house, but could it delicately match the bolt holes of wing and fuselage? Then the language problem arose. In disgust, I rested in the shade of an old shed at the edge of the strip. I nodded off to sleep thinking we would only succeed in pushing our hard-won wing through the fuselage. In my half-conscious state, I realised my engineers' chattering had stopped. Suddenly, the leading hand shook me and said, 'It's all right master, the wing's on. It fits like a glove.'"

Early in January 1950, Betsy was returned to service.

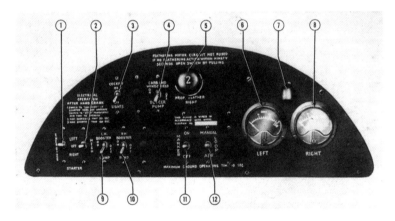

1. **Starter Energizing Switch**
2. **Starter Mesh Switch**
3. **Pilot Compartment Light Switch**
4. **Carburettor and Windshield Alcohol De-Icer Switch**
5. **Right Propeller Feathering Button**
6. **Left Ammeter**
7. **Panel Light**
8. **Right Ammeter**
9. **Left Fuel Booster Pump Switch**
10. **Right Fuel Booster Pump Switch**
11. **Marker Beacon Switch**
12. **Radio Compass Loop Antenna Switch**

CHINA NATIONAL AIRCRAFT CORPORATION'S (CNAC) Captain Hugh Woods was flying between Chungking and Chengdu when a gaggle of Japanese fighters swooped on his lumbering DC-3 (C-47). Their attack forced him to land at Suifu, and as he stood on the brakes their bombs blew off his starboard wing.

Expecting another raid, a gang of coolies pushed the plane three miles along a road and hid her in a copse. Hong Kong had no replacement wing, but they did have a spare DC-2 wing. Captain Harold Sweet lashed the wing to a stand-by aircraft's fuselage and rushed 900 miles to the rescue, where the legendary engineer "Sol" Soldinsky fitted it.

The boffins claimed that a wing five feet shorter than its sibling's aerodynamically could not fly, but with no book learning the DC-2 ½ revelled in its deformity and flew like a homing pigeon.

Betsy, in glorious technicolour, gracefully swoops over one of Hong Kong's many outer islands.

CHAPTER 11 : FAREWELL BETSY & NIKI — *The memories keep returning and each memory triggers a host of others.*

The Douglas Aircraft Co. Operations Manual for the DC-3.

I find myself thinking of how Betsy looked from the inside in 1947. It wasn't pretty. Long, indented metal benches ran the length of the cabin, with the longer one being on the starboard side. Each indent had a cushion, apparently offering some semblance of cleanliness, but this was a mere illusion. When one had a "leg-off", one would bundle them to form a couch that in appearance looked comfortable, but the first movement caused them to slide over the base metal surface. These benches could be lowered against the fuselage when passengers were wise enough to stay away.

Along the middle of the floor ran two loading tracks. When cargo was the prime load, it would be loaded and stabilised on a wooden platform with a rail that fitted into these tracks. Then it was secured with pins fore and aft as cargo was staggered to obtain the Centre of Gravity for safe-balance operation.

In Burma, we frequently combined cargo and passengers. I was aboard Betsy when low cargo ran the length of the fuselage. The more perceptive passengers used this as a footrest. At other times, it would be loaded at the rear bulkhead and of course prevented use of the toilet. Although this was tough on the elderly passengers, nobody seemed to mind.

In heavy rain, it was prudent to bring an umbrella or raincoat. I have been aboard when there was as much water sloshing around inside as there was outside. The pièce de résistance, however, was during thunderstorms, when the din bordered on the unbearable, and when lightning struck the scene was one taken directly from Dante's Inferno. With absolutely no soundproofing, the noise was frightful. To hold a

Chic demonstrates the generous legroom in Cathay's first economy-class cabins.

The well-padded interior of Betsy in 1947. Passenger unknown.

handsome first officer, Mike Russell. Their wedding closed down the airline for the day. Jean was the daughter of the amazing Major John Cannon who bought Cathay Pacific's abandoned Avro Anson and then persuaded Smithy Smith to get her airworthy. He escaped in her one moonless night with his wife and two dogs, having outwitted the Burmese secret police, who intended to execute an arrest warrant against him the next morning.

John was an astonishing man. He had a few hours' flying experience on small aircraft but none on an Anson. That flight, which ended in Butterworth, near Penang, has gone down in history. However, that has no part in this book and is told in *Syd's Last Pirate*.

Cathay Pacific continued to bring succour to inaccessible areas. In October, 1948, a Burmese newspaper recorded the completion of our 100th airdrop of rice, salt and flour. This notable delivery was to the starving people of Khaung-Laung-Hpu. Captain John Paish had trouble finding this tiny village for his map did not show it. All he knew was that it lay 200 miles north east of Myitkyina, nestling against forbidding Tibet. The district officer knew the area and spotted it immediately. That 100th food drop netted the company six US cents a pound per air mile. Had Cathay rediscovered the legendary lost gold of Ophir? The head-office accountants seemed to think so.

conversation showed that one had not only motivation but also fortitude bordering on the masochistic.

This reminds me of the recent 60th Cathay Pacific Anniversary Gala celebration. Sir Adrian Swire rushed up to me and from a distance of six inches screamed out, "Why are you not deaf?" This was a failing with early pilots who flew open-cockpit aircraft.

Anyhow, when I apologised for being so inconsiderate, he rushed off to badger another innocent victim.

I recall Cathay Pacific's first air hostess in Burma. This was Jean Cannon and the aircraft was Betsy. She would later marry our

Cathay Pacific commissioned the great Australian author, Alan Marshall, to prepare a booklet promoting its aerial travel. Here he sits in stony silence (right foreground) wondering what complimentary words could describe such spartan conditions; a potty in the aisle, a cargo-impeded toilet and miserably cramped passengers. Burma, 1948.

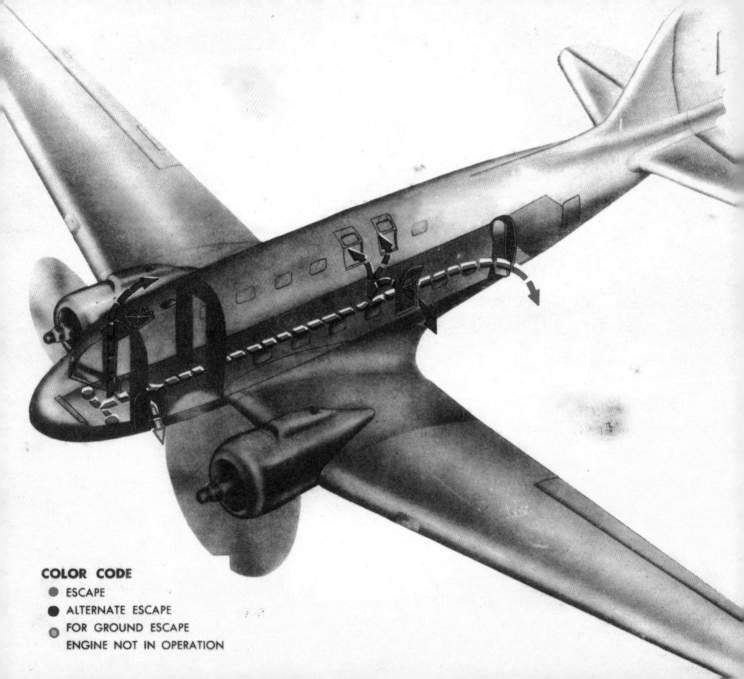

COLOR CODE

- ● ESCAPE
- ● ALTERNATE ESCAPE
- ● FOR GROUND ESCAPE
  ENGINE NOT IN OPERATION

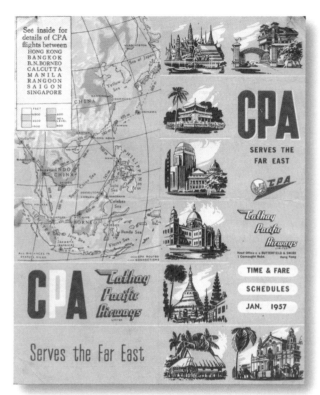

In the years that Betsy and Niki remained under Cathay Pacific Airways' stewardship, they had many other adventures. On August 6, 1955, Betsy was sold to Mandated Airlines of Lae, New Guinea for HK$320,000. There she would continue her love affair with adventure. She later went from Mandated to Ansett M.A.L. in 1963; then in 1970 to Ansett Papua New Guinea; in 1973 to Bush Pilots Airways Air Cargo and later still to Air Queensland Air Cargo.

The Hong Kong Civil Aviation deregistered Niki following her sale to Taiwan's Foshing Airways on July 25, 1961. Subsequently, the Royal Air Laos purchased and registered her as XW-TAE. Little is known of her career following that acquisition. Prior to this, she had, however, received one great honour. On September 12, 1958, she led the fly-past that officially opened Kai Tak airport's new Runway 13, the "Miracle Strip".

Betsy over Hong Kong Harbour, 1983. This historic picture shows Jardine House and Exchange Square (under construction) in the background. The Star Ferry Pier and Blake Pier have since been demolished.

ON SEPTEMBER 24, 1983, BETSY WAS RETURNED TO THE FOLD. It was, however, no easy task for the Cathay Pacific board had proved less than enthusiastic, and had shelved the project pleading that the cost far exceeded any possible gains. But then, deputy chairman of the parent Swire Group, Sir Adrian Swire, overruled. Capt. Martin Willing's dedication and determination had prevailed.

Following her return, Betsy became something of an unwelcome wanderer. Her last flight, a publicity exercise, took place the day following her arrival. Then engineers towed her to the rear of No.2 HAECO hangar, and removed her engines, instrument panel and wings. They covered her with dustsheets and forgot her. Meanwhile, the museum where she was to rest faced an unexpected building delay.

In 1986, to celebrate the 40th anniversary of Cathay Pacific Airways, HAECO refurbished Betsy, then barged her to Edinburgh Place, outside Hong Kong's City Hall in Central. On September 18, she was shown to the public and proved an enormous attraction.

In October, a planned visit by Queen Elizabeth II necessitated the return of Betsy to HAECO, whose engineers ignominiously hoisted her into the ceiling of one of their hangars. There she remained, neglected and unloved, until November 1989 when she was lifted into place in the then still incomplete Hong Kong Science Museum – her current and final resting place.

In 1998, Pacific Century Publishers Ltd produced the splendid *Wings Over Hong Kong*, narrated by the inimitable Julian Pettifer, in conjunction with the BBC. It proved a great success and caught the public's imagination for it recalled the gloriously romantic Kai Tak airport. Soon, the exciting 47-degree bank onto Runway 13 would be but a talking point by those who had experienced it to the envy of those who had not.

The project's producer invited me to be part of a day's filming. We moved onto the restricted area of the famous checkerboard that helped a pilot orientate himself during marginal weather. We then proceeded to a hill cemetery, which was the centre line of our 1946 approach.

We later arrived at the air-conditioned museum. As the floodlights hit the ceiling, there she was, suspended, and I spontaneously exclaimed: "Betsy – my love!"

Then I began to ponder just how much of the original plane actually hung there. I realised that wheels, tyres, engines, flight instruments, fuselage and cabin decor, and hundreds of rivets would have changed. By elimination, I determined just two parts, due to their simplicity, were probably

The refurbished Betsy was transported by barge to Edinburgh Place to celebrate Cathay Pacific's 40th anniversary in 1986.

the only originals – the flight yoke and rudder pedals.

At these simple controls, Pappy, Syd, Pinky Wawn, Nev Hemsworth, Peter Hoskins, Vic Leslie, Bob Donovan, John Riordan and others took on the vagaries of mother nature showing her worst traits. They guided Betsy through terrifying thunderheads and lightning that spawned hail that sandblasted the logo from the fuselage. With rain penetrating window seals, uniforms were soon soaked; meanwhile, valiant Betsy groaned as her straining engines drove her through a soaked atmosphere that had the intensity of a brick wall. With next to no navigational aids, the landing visibility was rarely more than minimal and frequently a mere memory.

The dreamer knows that once a hand embraces any material object it remains for eternity. Consequently, Betsy's yoke still carries the hand-print of some of the most brilliant pilots of that era - a time when the real history that became the Cathay Pacific Experience was created. And I was there.

In 1983, Betsy flew past the Peninsula Hotel just one more time.

CPA pilot Capt. Lawrie King gets the customary HAECO greeting. "HAEC staff positively bend over backwards to provide the service the customer requires," says King.

"**W**ORKING WITH HAECO WAS ALWAYS A BREEZE, THE CHAPS WERE ALWAYS WILLING TO GO THE EXTRA DISTANCE FOR US."

The Hong Kong Aircraft Engineering Company came into being on November 1, 1950 – or at least that is HAECO's official birth date. The company is, however, rather older, since HAECO was the product of a union between two rival companies formed at Hong Kong's Kai Tak airport immediately after World War II: the Pacific Air Maintenance & Supply Company (PAMAS) and Jardine Air Maintenance Company (JAMCo), owned respectively by two British trading companies – Swire and Jardine.

Jardine Matheson was established in Canton (Guangzhou) in 1832. John Swire & Sons, formed in Liverpool in 1816, opened its first China house in Shanghai in 1866. Amongst the leading foreign hongs on the China coast in the late nineteenth century, Ewo ("Happy Harmony") and Taikoo ("Great and Ancient"), the Chinese names by which the two firms are known to this day, were keen rivals in a number of fields, their businesses revolving primarily around shipping. After World War II, both companies diversified into aviation: Jardine forming Hong Kong Airways in 1947 and Swire taking a controlling interest in Cathay Pacific Airways in 1948. The two firms established their own aircraft-maintenance facilities in 1946 and 1947 respectively.

After the merger of JAMCo and PAMAS, Jardine's interest in HAECO – or HAEC as the new company was at first known – gradually waned. Twenty-five per cent of the shares were floated on the Hong Kong stock market in 1965, and in 1975 HAECO became a member of the Swire Group, when Swire Pacific increased its shareholding to 51 per cent. Today, Swire Pacific has a 32.8 per cent direct shareholding in HAECO, while associate company Cathay Pacific Airways has a 27.45 per cent shareholding.

In addition to its substantial shareholding in HAECO, Cathay Pacific has, from its earliest days, been HAECO's principal customer. The history of the Hong Kong Aircraft Engineering Company is thus intricately bound up with the development of Cathay from shoestring regional operator to leading international carrier. The growth of the airline from a single DC-3, Betsy, to the current fleet of 65 wide-body Boeing and Airbus aircraft, has always had, and continues to have, a decisive influence on the way HAECO's capabilities and facilities have developed.

A 1950's picture of Betsy at Kai Tak airport.

IT WAS DECIDED THAT BRINGING A C-47, CATHAY'S FIRST TYPE OF AIRCRAFT, TO CATHAY PACIFIC CITY, WOULD BE A SPLENDID WAY TO MARK THE AIRLINE'S 60TH ANNIVERSARY. Betsy, of course, was the ideal choice, but she was firmly wired in place at the Hong Kong Science Museum. The Chief Curator, Chee Kuen Yip, and his Senior Technical Officer, Chi Kin Wong, would not consider her removal.

Thoughts then turned to Niki, but investigations indicated that in all probability she no longer existed. Consequently, in mid-September 2005, Engineering Director Derek Cridland and General Manager Engineering Technical Steve Chadwick began to look for another C-47.

This brought Dave Price and Steve Danks into the quest. Steve was familiar with aircraft prospects in the Philippines, while Dave had extensive experience in moving old aircraft. After some brief persuasion, Simon Mayes, a Cathay Senior Maintenance Controller, joined the team.

Several companies around the world were approached for vintage C-47s, the most promising being CM Aviation based in Manila. There the choice of two suitable C-47s was narrowed to RP-C1101. She was built by Douglas at Long Beach, California for the USAAF as the C-47A-30-DL Skytrain 42-23663 in May 1943. This put her in the correct age group as a suitable replacement for the original Niki.

The restless South China Sea now came into their consideration. Should they ship her to Hong Kong or chance flying her? Although RP-C1101 looked good, could she handle the five-hour flight to Hong Kong?

On the eve of the Chinese New Year in 2006, Derek Cridland authorised the payment of a deposit, and on February 1, RP-C1101 was earmarked for Cathay. At this point, Mark Sutch, Cathay Operations Manager and one-time Country Manager Philippines, took an active part in the operational and flight-planning part of the project. Mark, working closely with the Hong Kong Civil Aviation Department (CAD), created the catalyst that brought the project to fruition within the tight time schedule.

Although the deposit was paid, nobody had seen her fly. On February 6, Dave Price and Steve Danks returned to Manila and before noon were aboard RP-C1101 for a touch-and-go at Clark Air Force Base. The trip satisfied them and they reported that she

The replica NIKI stands sentinel outside the CX Headquarters at HK International Airport.

A group of CPA air hostesses qualify for St John Ambulance badges in the early 1950's. The lucky man in the centre is the doctor in charge of their course.

handled well and was mechanically sound. They hastened back to Hong Kong to report that the project was feasible, and subsequently the delivery flight was set for February 20.

The ferry crew was Derek Cridland (Engineering Director), Steve Chadwick (General Manager Engineering Technical), Captain John McCormick (General Manager Flying), and Rob Wales (Manager Maintenance Support). Delay in departure occurred when several release signatures were needed, but before long they were 8,000 feet above the treacherous South China Sea in a 63-year-old aircraft on their way to Hong Kong.

Four hours and 50 minutes after take-off, they emerged from low cloud to land at Chek Lap Kok, having recreated a trip that the original Niki had regularly flown back in 1946.

1946 - 1954

1954 - 1969

1969 - 1983

1983 - 1990

1990 - 1999

1999 - current

1999 - current

CPA crew badges over the years.

117

"**F**LYING A DC-3 AGAIN FOR THE FIRST TIME – STARTING UP THE FIRST ENGINE, IT MADE THE MOST SATISFACTORY RUMBLE.**" Early in 2006, I found myself at Manila Airport, sitting in a DC-3 cockpit staring at dials and gauges that had just about become museum pieces and wondering what this thing was going to be like to fly.

Would it prove to be a beast of a machine, hell-bent on showing that a 50-year-old ex-fighter pilot who traipses around the world in a modern-day Boeing aircraft was "easy meat" or would it be the loved and respected "Gooney Bird" of my father's era, which reportedly had not a malicious bone in its well-riveted body? There was only one way to find out. So, with great aplomb, or as much as it was possible to muster, I started the first of the Pratt & Whitney engines. I must say it made the most satisfactory rumble and it was quite obvious that, whatever this aircraft had done in its life, whatever events had raised the eyebrows and heart rates of its wartime pilots – and I am sure there would have been many of those – and however doggedly this DC-3 had been forced to make itself continue to fly, there remained two things: one, that a considerable "willingness" existed in this slightly aged queen; and two, that there still could be aroused the spirit of true aviation – that something could generate that pure delight of feeling the aircraft come alive as you get airborne.

The sun blazed on the glass windscreen and the heated air added to the aroma of an almost bygone, romantic era of aviation. The smells of hydraulic fluid, engine oil and good old-fashioned aviation fuel (flying "petrol" as opposed to jet fuel) combined with the solid earthy-home smell of the aircraft itself delivered the message that this aircraft was from a time when aircraft were meant to do one thing and one thing only: FLY.

As we lifted off in the dazzling sunlight, I was instantly reminded of all the fantastic aspects of flying. It took me straight back to when I started in aviation; when all was new and just plain unbelievably good fun. The DC-3 proved to be a true, honest aircraft that wanted to keep on flying and wanted you, the pilot, to know it. It was marvellous stuff and something that I did not want to end. This was no "gentleman's carriage" meant for fine days and light winds; no, this was an all-business aircraft, made to do a job and made to do it well, with little given to luxury in the cockpit and certainly no comparison to the clinical sterility of today's transport aircraft. Alas, I was sure that this ability to raise the "spirit of aviation" existed only in the old and bygone aircraft and was an art lost to today's manufacturers.

I recalled, however, a previous occasion when I had sat in an unfamiliar cockpit. That had been in an aircraft at the other end of its life. Not one destined for perhaps one or two last adventures as this DC-3 was, but one that was just starting its life. The last time I had been sitting in an unfamiliar cockpit had been some years previously in the Boeing 777, during that aircraft's development programme, and the differences between the two machines seemed extreme. But when I recall the feeling of lifting the Boeing 777 into the air, I now realise where the delight in flying that aircraft comes from. I just did not know it at the time as I had not experienced it for years, but it was and is the exact same feelings generated by a proud old aircraft on a hot summer day in Manila. And not many aircraft, old or new, can do that.

CAPT. J. McCORMICK

The original NIKI in front of the HAECO hangar.

NIKI HEADS FOR HOME. At this point, Simon Mayes, Steve Danks and I had to make a run to the international terminal of Manila Airport for our 'Jumbo' to Hong Kong. Our flight time would be 95 minutes. The crew on RP-C1101 (Niki) had 4 hours 50 minutes ahead of them in a classic aircraft. John McCormick later said he saw us over-fly him at our cruise altitude of 37,000 feet while he was at 8,000 feet. Steve-D and I would have swapped our first-class seats in a flash!

We arrived in plenty of time at Chek Lap Kok but the visibility was not good. It was OK for a 747 with its state-of-the-art avionics, but RP-C1101 had been flying visual all her life. With this in mind, we drove up to the Hong Kong Aircraft Engineering Company (HAECO) hangar.

There we met up with Mark Sutch and a large welcoming team from Cathay Pacific and HAECO.

Mark had with him a hand-held VHF radio, which allowed us to listen in to the approach frequency. We knew she was in the circuit when the air-traffic controller said: "Dragonair A330 speed up on your approach as you have a real aircraft behind you. It's a DC-3," together with "Cathay 777 please slow to 140 knots as the classic aircraft ahead of you will be the first to land."

Out of the low cloud came the landing lights and the familiar sound. She landed long on the main runway, but still took five minutes to taxi to the maintenance area. All on board had a fantastic experience that they will remember for years to come.

RP-C1101 had joined one of the most modern fleets in the world and she looked spectacular among the Cathay Airbuses and Boeings. We all had a secret tear in our eyes over the achievement. The first good night's sleep for weeks lay ahead.

DAVE PRICE

Niki lookalike comes to Hong Kong.

FULL CIRCLE ON TWO ENGINES. Cathay Pacific Airways today operates a growing fleet of Boeing 777-300ERs, which are the backbone of its North American services. These fuel-efficient twinjets – the world's largest – fly farther than early-model 747s and carry just as many passengers. They also bring this world-renowned airline back to its roots because Cathay started out as a twin-engine operator more than six decades ago.

World War II had just ended when two adventurous fliers, a Yank and an Aussie, formed Cathay Pacific Airways in Hong Kong in September 1946. For their airplane, Roy Farrell and Sydney de Kantzow turned to the trusty Douglas C-47 Skytrain, a military derivative of the legendary DC-3 airliner of the late 1930s.

The global airline industry grew up with the DC-3, whose magic combination of performance and economics let carriers earn solid profits without subsidies for the first time in history. On the eve of World War II, DC-3s were carrying 90 percent of U.S. air traffic and much of the rest of the world's as well.

During the war, C-47s island-hopped across the world's oceans to let the Allies stage logistically all around the world. From tropical atolls to Arctic tundra on skis, these "Gooney Birds" – or Dakotas as British and Commonwealth forces called them – made themselves right at home in every corner of the globe. They even conquered the Himalayas, delivering vast amounts of fuel, ammunition and other supplies into China.

Farrell and de Kantzow, both veteran "Hump" pilots, knew the Douglas C-47 well. Here was a money-making airplane that could operate in and out of unimproved airfields and haul virtually any load that could be manhandled through its cargo doors. Purchasing two war-surplus examples that they named Betsy and Niki, they began operations.

Those first airliners left a lot to be desired in terms of passenger comfort. Their bare-bones military interiors offered fold-down, aluminum-frame-and-canvas bench seating along the cabin side walls, so passengers sat facing inward to stare at cargo lashed to the floor. Greater comfort came with later C-47s in the young airline's fleet, which were converted to plush DC-3 configuration with 21 forward-facing passenger seats.

These propeller twins cruised at a leisurely 150 knots (278 km/h) and flew up to 1,400 nautical miles (2,500 km) non-stop. They made Cathay profitable from the outset, and the airline was soon linking Hong Kong with Manila, Singapore, Bangkok, a variety of Chinese mainland destinations, and other regional ports of call.

In 1953, meantime, the United States passed landmark regulations restricting two- and three-engine airliners to routes that remained at all times within one hour's flight time (at one-engine-inoperative cruise speed) of an alternate airport. The rest of the world quickly followed suit, effectively banning twins like the DC-3, plus any old trimotors still in service, from over-water or other routes more safely served by four-engine types like the Douglas DC-6B or Lockheed Constellation.

Given the limited reliability of piston engines and propellers, this 60-minute rule was a good idea. More engines definitely provided greater safety in the propeller era. But starting in the late 1950s, the industry underwent a rapid transition to turbine propulsion that brought about a quantum leap in engine reliability. Further gains came with the introduction and ongoing improvement of high-bypass-ratio turbofan technology. As a result, today's modern fanjets are at least 100 times more reliable than the large piston aero engines of the late 1950s.

By 1964, this rising propulsion reliability – one of aviation's most dramatic trends – saw three-engine jets exempted from the 60-minute rule. In 1985, it allowed ETOPS flying to begin. Standing for extended operations, ETOPS is of course the global regulatory framework under which the world's airlines have long operated two-engine jetliners on routes that take the airplane beyond one hour of an airport. Enormously successful, ETOPS sets the highest standard for safe, reliable flight operations. It is the state of the art in long-haul air travel.

The Boeing 777 offers a good example of what has been collectively achieved over the decades. As of this writing, more than 700 of these big twins are in service, powered by Rolls-Royce, Pratt & Whitney or GE fanjets. Regardless of which engine type adorns its wings, however, a 777 will on average log about 25,000 flights and spend well over 100,000 hours aloft between in-flight engine failures or precautionary shutdowns. Most 777s will never reach these thresholds before being retired from service after many decades aloft.

For airline pilots just starting out today, this astonishing propulsion reliability means that they have a reasonable expectation of flying an entire career without ever experiencing an engine failure. Nevertheless, line pilots of course train for them!

Cathay Pacific Airways has come full circle with its Boeing 777-300ER ETOPS fleet. Rugged and reliable, these workhorse twin-engine jets carry to new heights the enduring legacy of Betsy and Niki.

CAPT. CHESTER L. "CHET" EKSTRAND

Boeing Vice President Chet Ekstrand is a former USAF fighter pilot and air-transport-rated pilot. Formerly the chief of flight training for Boeing Commercial Airplanes, he is well known in the global airline community.

Date	Type of Machine	Number of Machine	Duration of Flight	Character of Flight	Pilot	PASSENGERS	REMARKS
					SEPT. 1947 CATHAY	PACIFIC AIRWAYS HONGKONG	
1	C-47	HDG VR	4.4	O	LEWIS - SELF	LOUTTIT	HONGKONG - MANILA INST .5 WEATHER
2	C-47	HDG VR	4.9	O	,, ,,	,,	MANILA - CANTON INST 2.0
2	C-47	HDG VR	1.4	O	,, ,,	,,	SWEAT JOB CANTON - HONGKONG INST .5
14	PBY-5A	HDG VR	1:20	O	SELF		Test Hop
16	,,	,,	7:30	O	,,		Hongkong to Saigon
17	,,	,,	7:00	O	,,		Saigon to Macao
18	,,	,,	:48	O	,,		Macao to Hongkong
18	,,	,,	7:05	O	,,		Hongkong to Manila
19	,,	,,	5:35	O	,,		Manila to Macao
19	,,	,,	:35	O	,,		Macao to Hongkong
29	,,	,,	6:50	O	,,		Hongkong to Bangkok
	Brought forward	2353:50					
	Air month	47:01					
	Total time to date	2400:51					

The logbook of Capt. Dale Cramer, the courageous softly spoken pilot whose flight deck I was privileged to share, for September, 1947.
Entries record flights by C-47 and PBY (Catalina) to SE Asian destinations.

ACKNOWLEDGEMENTS — *I have long held the view that a contributor can be one who promotes the success of any work by merely expressing enthusiasm and showing support and friendship. Each name that follows fulfils those criteria and shares my grateful thanks:*

Moe Alkaff, Master of Ceremony supreme; Gordon Andreassend, a thoughtful man who is comfortable encouraging others; James Barrington, a reserved man who adores cricket; Mark Beaumont – the Dark Moment, who flew from the States to be my Presenter; Liz Bosher, Martin Craigs' right hand; Capt. "Cam" Cameron, my chaperone at the celebration of Captains on Probation; Steve Chadwick, GM Engineering Technical; Daniel Chan, Marketing & Sales Coordinator SIN; Philip Chen, the very likeable and astute Cathay CE; Dane Cheng, General Manager Corporate Communication; Martin Craigs, the dedicated President of the Aerospace Forum (Asia); Derek Cridland, Engineering Director; Chris Donnolley, Asst Communication Services Manager; Charles Doyle, a canny man who sees through any subterfuge; Cliff Dunnaway, enthusiastic manager of the Hong Kong Historical Aircraft Association; Elizabeth "Liz" Eather, my daughter-in-law and proofreader; Capt. Tony Fung, a Chinese Cathay aviation success; Robert Gibson, my advisor and motivator; John Hewson, my proofreader; Ian Johnson, a dedicated aviation researcher; Darryn Johnston, FLEXintegrated Marketing SIN; Tracey Kwong, my thoughtful CX minder; Yip Kan Kenneth Law, an aspiring Cathay captain; Geok Hong Lim, Personnel & Admin. Manager and my Singapore minder; Norman Lo, Director of Civil Aviation Hong Kong , and a man of his word; Mitch Lovett, a painter of dignity and charm; Capt. John McCormick, a superb aviator, comfortable on any flight deck; Kerry McGlynn, we hail from the same Sydney suburb; David Price, instrumental in bringing the replica Niki back; Nick Rhodes, my mate, and introducer; Charlie Stewart-Cox, a generous, thoughtful individual; Mark Sutch, a worthy chip off the old chopstick; Helen Tan, Confidential Secretary SIN; Mark Tindall, the popular CX World editor; Tony Tyler, a long-time and valued friend; Capt. Martin Willing, former Cathay B747 skipper and aviation historian of proven ability; Stephen Wong, Country Manager Singapore and gentleman; Terence Wu, Financial Services Manager SIN.

INDEX

INDEX

INDEX

INDEX

A 14-cylinder, twin-row, radial air-cooled, super-charged piston engine used in many DC-3 and C-47 aircraft.

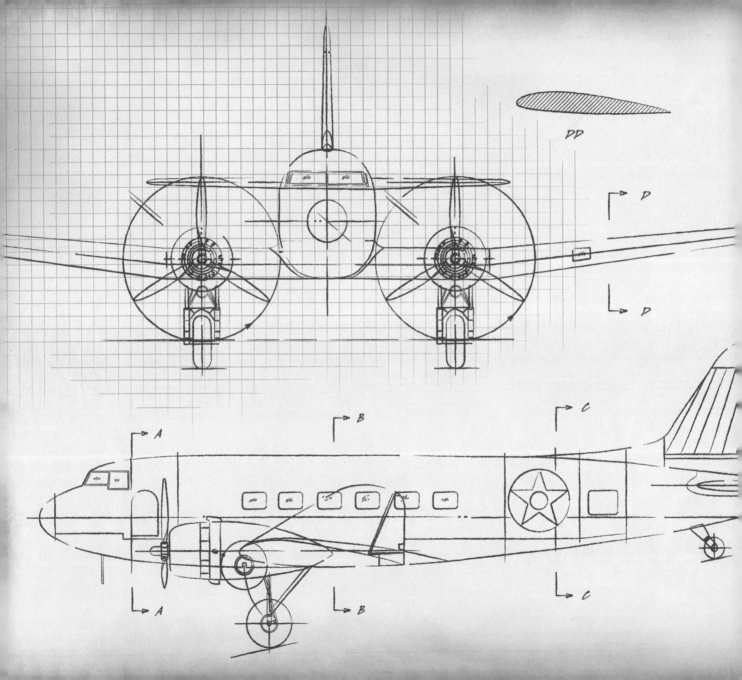

DD

D

D

A

A

B

B

C

C